simply vegetarian cookbook

simply vegetarian cookbook

FUSS-FREE RECIPES EVERYONE WILL LOVE

SUSAN PRIDMORE

creator of *The Wimpy Vegetarian* blog

foreword by AMANDA HESSER and MERRILL STUBBS
co-founders of FOOD52

ROCKRIDGE
PRESS

Design: Eliza Bullock
Editor: Stacy Wagner-Kinnear
Production Editor: Erum Khan
Cover Photography © Barol16/iStock
Back Cover Photography © Jennifer Davick, S_Karau/Shutterstock, Marija Vidal/Food styling by Cregg Green.
Photography © Marija Vidal/Food styling by Cregg Green, p. 45, 59, 70, 91; Jennifer Davick, p.ii; Vera Lair/Stocksy, p.v; Sophia Hsin/Stocksy, xiv; Jennifer Davick, p.20; Shebeko/ Shutterstock, p.42; S_Karau/Shutterstock, p.146; Amawasri Pakdara/Shutterstock, p.180.

ISBN: Print 978-1-64152-000-3 | eBook 978-1-64152-001-0

To Myles,
my Carnivorous Maximus husband,
who gave this book wings.

CONTENTS

FOREWORD

AS OMNIVORES, WE LOVE that this book doesn't make us feel judged or less than. Instead, it has us curious and intrigued. Perhaps this is because Susan is upfront about the challenge of navigating dinner with her husband Myles (who is "mostly carnivore") and advocates for compromise over standoff (her vegetarian main dishes often become his sides).

Or maybe it's because her mantra to simplify and add flexibility to vegetarian cooking makes it way more accessible to people like us. Don't get us wrong, we love our vegetables—we just don't like being told they're all we can eat and that we shouldn't give into our urges for gloriously juicy, fatty meat once in a while. But Susan is the opposite of tyrannical, gently advising newcomers to "start with one or two veggie dinners a week and build from there."

Or perhaps we were won over by the intuitive way Susan chose to organize this book—by cooking method rather than dish type—which speaks to our natural rhythms as cooks and does a lot of the decision-making for us by automatically taking into consideration crucial factors like time, seasonality, and equipment needs.

In the No Cook chapter, Susan offers stand-alone dishes like smoothies and wraps as well as an abundance of vibrant salads, including an edamame, corn, and red pepper number with lots of fresh herbs that you assemble in a mason jar. Who, we ask, could argue with that?

The One Pot and Skillet section delivers gold on the egg front (you heard it here first: Spicy Skillet Eggs with beans and avocado just may be the next shakshuka) and delves deep into noodle territory with Easy Miso Ramen, Chickpea Bolognese, and a zippy Roasted Red Pepper Pasta.

Aside from the utter lack of pretension, what we love about this book is the pure focus on making the most of seasonal ingredients by layering in flavor while still keeping things honest and straightforward. We were won over by Susan's suggestion to use chopped olives and oregano to transform a simple dish of pasta and chickpeas into something briny and fragrant; this is just the sort of brilliant but unfussy attention to detail that ensures this combination will make its way into our weekly rotation.

If we're being totally honest, we're probably more in Myles's camp than Susan's. But what we love about the *Simply Vegetarian Cookbook* is that it's just as much a book for us as it is for the committed vegetarian cook. We think of it as a dear friend whose first language is home cook, but who also happens to be fluent in vegetarian.

AMANDA HESSER and MERRILL STUBBS
Co-founders of Food52

SPICY SKILLET EGGS (PAGE 104)

INTRODUCTION

LIFE USED TO BE EASY. Well, at least as far as dinner went. I'd fire up the grill after a long day at work, massage a spice mix into some meat, and watch over it as the smell of charred fat filled the air. Steamy hot corn on the cob slathered in garlic butter and a simple salad tossed with a zippy vinaigrette came next. Dinner was on the table in less than 30 minutes. No stress. No extensive planning. Easy peasy.

Then one of us graduated from culinary school—that would be me—and decided to go vegetarian. For a brief moment, I blithely imagined my husband, Myles, sharing this adventure with me. In just-as-brief a moment, Myles asked me, "Are you kidding?" in a tone that sounded a lot like "Are you *crazy*?" It would be fun, I cajoled, to explore the worlds of quinoa and tofu together. But one of us—that would be Myles—thought there was good reason for not exploring those worlds. "I need meat. If I wasn't supposed to eat it, I wouldn't have incisors," he argued.

For the first month, Myles eyed the bunches of kale coming into the house with grave suspicion and staked out his meaty base of operations on a single refrigerator shelf. Swiss chard and mustard greens soon expanded into kale's territory, with long, frilly arms spilling out of biodegradable plastic bags. After careful assessment, Myles and his incisors took over another shelf to shore up the ranks. Pork chops, ground beef, and every cut of steak available were drafted into service to beat back the onslaught of the greens. By the third month, our turf war was reeling out of control, and I threatened to lease a meat locker a few miles from our home.

Detente was declared with cheese as the peacemaker. With the addition of cheese, Myles reacted with, if not enthusiasm, at least acceptance. He still eyed me suspiciously when he saw a pot of grains simmering on the stove, but the objections softened over time, and we began to share—and even enjoy—some dishes together again while we each waited for the other to come to their senses. We found common ground with herbed goat cheese melting into warm farro and asparagus salads, and garlicky kale and roasted tomatoes nestled in Cheddar cheese galette crusts.

My biggest challenge in undertaking a vegetarian diet was the sudden need to actually plan a meal that would be balanced, healthy, and satisfying for us both. No longer could I start to think about dinner at 6:00 p.m. and throw something together on the fly—at least not in the beginning. And I wasn't interested in using more pots and pans than any person should even own just to make a nightly dinner for two.

That was seven years ago. Today, I'm mostly vegetarian. I eat some fish, especially when eating out, and Myles is mostly carnivore, usually having my vegetarian entrée as his side dish. I still use some dairy, but cheese has migrated from its peacemaker role to a cameo just before serving. I now lean more heavily on a supporting pantry of herbs and easy-to-make flavor enhancers to punch up flavor and texture, (mostly) without the fat. My favorite flavor enhancers are included in Chapter 8: Kitchen Staples (page 167). Having these stars on hand also makes quick work of last-minute dinners and keeps them healthy.

My goals in both our kitchen and this book are to share the following:

- Accessible, healthy recipes sporting a limited number of ingredients you can easily find, many of which you likely already have on hand.
- Mostly main dishes that won't take you all day to make (unless you're using a slow cooker, but in that case the slow cooker is doing the work), along with time-saving preparation tips.
- Dishes that can be easily adjusted for different diets. Although all of the recipes are 100 percent vegetarian, I include variations so you can add fish, poultry, or red meat if you're cooking for others who would appreciate (or even demand!) those additions.
- The kitchen appliances that can make your vegetarian life easier.

Whether you're cooking for strict vegetarians, both vegetarians and omnivores, or you just want to include healthy meatless dishes in your weekly menus—and whether you're cooking for yourself or a dinner party of 10—these recipes will work as well in your kitchen as they have in mine. There are enough things to be stressed about in life. Dinner shouldn't be one of them.

1
MEATLESS MADE EASY

IF YOU'RE CONSIDERING a more vegetarian diet, congratulations! There are many reasons to make this change, but remember that change doesn't have to be either absolute or immediate. To the contrary, the biggest, most lasting changes I've made in my life have been ones done in incremental steps. After long periods of skipping the gym, I don't immediately launch into running on the treadmill, doing Pilates, and lifting weights seven days a week. If I did, I'd likely spend the next week in bed (or the emergency room), which accomplishes nothing. Diet changes are similar.

To ensure this decision takes firm root in your life, I recommend starting with one or two veggie dinners a week and building from there. Or maybe you'll decide to stay there, if that's what feels right for your body. Whatever level of commitment you choose, it's best to start with easy meals that don't require you to completely reorganize your life just to put dinner on the table. This book is full of recipes that can help you do just that and more. Welcome!

STARTING SOMETHING NEW

A vegetarian diet embraces fruits, vegetables, grains, and seeds, as well as protein-packed legumes, soy-based foods, eggs, and dairy products. In other words, it includes a huge variety of foods. Whether you're switching your diet completely or just eating one veggie meal a week, consider this an invitation to try a new vegetable you've walked by at the market, or a new way to prepare a familiar food (like cauliflower—arguably the most versatile vegetable on the planet). Your next (or first) vegetarian meal can be pasta tossed with vegetables and covered with cheese, but it can also be so much more.

Regardless of whether you go Paleo, Whole30, vegetarian, or adopt any other eating plan, there's research involved once the euphoria of making the decision evaporates. At the top of the list is determining which foods are compatible with the new way of eating you've chosen to pursue. But that's just the beginning. Other core considerations include:

- How to eat a balanced diet on your new meal program, and determining what that means.
- Figuring out new meals to cook that everyone at the table will like, when you barely have time to cook the dishes you already know.
- Learning about new ingredients—how to prep, cook, and store them—and whether they'll fit into your budget.
- What to eat for lunch at work, especially if your office doesn't have a kitchen.

These are familiar challenges to both the longtime vegetarian and someone taking their first steps into vegetarianism, and this book was created to help you conquer those challenges. I may not resolve every obstacle you run into, but I hope to make your road much smoother. You shouldn't feel defeated before you've even begun.

EASY FOR EVERYONE

This cookbook is filled with recipes that are easy to make, without using every pan you own and spice in your cabinet just to get dinner on the table. It's intended for vegetarians cooking for themselves at the end of a long workday, as well as for home cooks preparing family meals for both vegetarians and omnivores. To support a mixed family table like mine, Flexitarian tips for adding meat or fish are offered with many recipes.

Many of the recipes are ideal for busy weeknights, but if you find some of them a little too time-consuming or involved, look for Make it Ahead tips, or leave them for the weekend when you're not as pressed for time.

Easy to Make

Included in the book are a handful of snacks, side dishes, and breakfasts, but since most recipes are designed for lunch or dinner, the chapters are organized by category of easiness instead of type of meal. Here's a lineup of the chapters:

NO COOK offers recipes that may call for precooked food, like a can of chickpeas, but won't require you to cook anything. Some of the Flexitarian tips suggest adding cooked meat or seafood, but of course they're optional.

THIRTY MINUTES MAX includes recipes that can be executed from prepping to serving in 30 minutes or less.

FIVE INGREDIENTS provides dishes made with no more than five ingredients, not including cooking oil or butter, water, salt, and black pepper.

ONE POT & SKILLET and **SHEET PAN & BAKING DISH** both highlight recipes for all-in-one meals that keep the kitchen (mostly) clean.

SLOW COOKER & PRESSURE COOKER serves up hands-off meals than can be made with either piece of equipment, or sometimes both.

KITCHEN STAPLES is where you'll find pantry items you can make ahead to add flavor to food and speed up meal prep during the week.

Some recipes fall into more than one category, which is inevitable, and tough decisions had to be made. In the end, I placed them in the chapter that makes them a standout.

Easy to Adapt

Taking on additional work just to figure out what to make for dinner can halt dietary changes quicker than a New Year's resolution. If it's not easy, it simply won't last past the initial excitement.

The first step in facing down the dinner challenge is to start by making your favorite dishes without meat or fish, and make simple meat substitutions. For example, make your favorite chili vegetarian by adding an extra can of black beans in place of the meat. Try tofu, tempeh, or seitan on your next fajita night without adjusting any seasonings. You may be surprised how easy it is.

The next step is to experiment a little, using this cookbook of recipes that range from easy to moderately easy. In case you're juggling more than one dietary consideration, every recipe in this book highlights whether it's dairy-free, gluten-free, nut-free, and/or vegan, and many include recommendations for adapting the recipes to these diets. And even if your table doesn't include any vegetarians, there's no reason they can't fully enjoy these recipes just as they are.

Easy to Find

Just because you want to shift the way you eat shouldn't mean you have to research and track down ingredients you've never heard of. The vast majority of the ingredients used in this cookbook's recipes are ones you should be able to find year-round in your local market, with some being available only when they're in season. But a handful of ingredients that I include are ones you may need to order online (like I do), but are worth the extra step. For example, the Better Than Bouillon product line adds a depth of flavor to broth-based dishes without having to add a long list of additional ingredients.

THE BALANCED VEGETARIAN PLATE

I eat a wide variety of fresh, in-season fruits and vegetables and head to the frozen food section when needed. But when I switched to a more vegetarian diet, I worried whether I was getting enough protein. Then I worried that I was eating too many carbs.

Protein is essential for repairing cells and making new ones, and amino acids are its building blocks. Of the 20 different amino acids we need every day, there are nine that our body can't manufacture on its own. A "complete protein" is a food that delivers all nine of these amino acids. With the notable exception of soy beans, no fruit or vegetable meets this test, so they must be combined with another food to deliver the full protein package by the end of the day. This gave birth to the adage "a grain, a green, and a bean" to define the balanced vegetarian plate.

For carbs and fat, my own approach is everything in moderation. I keep a pantry of spices to kick up flavor and texture. I eat grains and legumes most days, but not too much. I add a fried egg to vegetable dishes, but not every day, and occasionally have tofu.

Omega-3s

If fish (and, to a lesser extent, red meats) are the most powerful sources of omega-3 fatty acids, where can vegetarians and vegans get their daily dose? Here are a few great foods that supply omega-3s, with some additional health benefits to boot.

- Flaxseeds are high in fiber, support digestive health, and help lower cholesterol.

- Chia seeds are small but mighty: They're loaded with fiber, protein, antioxidants, and micronutrients.

- Walnuts boost bone health, improve metabolism, and help control diabetes.

- Beans, particularly navy and kidney beans, as well as cannellini beans, are excellent sources for fiber, help lower cholesterol, reduce heart disease risk, and control blood sugar.

POWER PROTEINS

It's not difficult to get enough protein every day as a vegetarian, particularly if you eat soy-based foods, but it's important to know what foods pack the greatest protein punch. When I began this journey, I wasn't a fan of tofu (it was all about the texture), and had never even tried its cousin tempeh. Finding ways to marinate tofu and make it crispy went a long way to making me a bigger fan, and I found it was easy to add to sauces and casseroles without anyone being the wiser.

Here are some of the top protein foods compatible with a vegetarian diet. I list the amount of protein per suggested serving size and include ideas for what meats they can replace, if applicable. Some of these foods in the table aren't meat substitutes; they are just healthy protein sources to add to many dishes. I call them my Power Proteins PP .

PROTEIN SOURCE	PROTEIN AMOUNT	SWAP OPPORTUNITY
⅓ cup seitan	21 grams	Chicken, pork, beef
1 cup tempeh	31 grams	Chicken, pork, beef
1 cup tofu	20 grams	Chicken, pork, fish
½ cup peanut butter PP	32 grams	N/A
1 large egg	7 grams	Chicken, pork, beef
1 cup Greek yogurt PP	18 grams	N/A
1 cup cooked chickpeas or black beans	15 to 16 grams	Chicken, pork, beef
1 cup edamame, shelled PP	17 grams	N/A
1 cup cooked lentils	18 grams	Pork, beef
¼ cup whole almonds PP	8 grams	N/A
2 tablespoons nutritional yeast	8 grams	Cheese

CARB SWAPS

Ah, carbohydrates. High-carb meals are often a vegetarian go-to for dinners—so filling, so satisfying. But not necessarily healthy. If eating healthier goes hand in hand with why you're eating more vegetarian meals, it's good to know that many vegetables are excellent carb substitutes: witness the popularity of zucchini noodles (zoodles) and cauliflower-crust pizzas. Check out your local market for containers of zoodles, or buy a spiralizer and make your own. Purchase a bag of frozen cauliflower "rice" to stand in for grains, or grate your own using a box grater or a food processor. For a knife-and-fork veggie burger, swap out a bun for two portabella mushroom caps. The possibilities are endless.

Although this cookbook isn't specifically designed to be low carb, there are enough ideas sprinkled throughout to avoid the dangers of getting stuck in a rut of grains, beans, and pasta. Some of my favorite swaps are listed below, along with a comparison of carb amounts.

FOOD	CARBS	LOW-CARB SWAP	CARBS
1 cup cooked spaghetti	14 grams	1 cup zucchini noodles	3.7 grams
1 cup cooked brown rice	45 grams	1 cup cauliflower rice	5 grams
1 cup cooked spaghetti	14 grams	1 cup spaghetti squash	7 grams
1 tortilla	98 grams	1 lettuce leaf	1 gram
1 cup cooked black beans	13 grams	1 cup tofu	4.6 grams
1 hamburger bun	29 grams	2 portabella mushrooms	1 gram

VERSATILE VEGGIES

In the vast world of vegetables, you need to know your most valuable players. My favorites are those that are readily available year-round and can be used in a variety of ways to punch up flavors and nutrition. Here are my top 11, and why I almost always have them on hand.

CAULIFLOWER This is *the* white food to eat. In addition to its robust nutritional profile, it plays well with other veggies and spices, and can be riced, puréed, chopped into soups, sliced into steaks, or layered in casseroles.

CHICKPEAS These are loaded with protein, and you can roast them with spices for a snack, whip them up for some hummus, or mash them for "meatballs." White kidney (cannellini) beans are a great substitute for chickpeas, if you prefer them.

BUTTERNUT SQUASH It isn't fall without butternut squash soup, but this vegetable can also be spiralized into noodles, thinly sliced and layered in lasagna, or sliced in half and roasted. It also doubles as the perfect bowl for a mixture of grains, dried fruits, and other vegetables. Acorn squash halves make great bowls, too.

ZUCCHINI Grate zucchini and fold into baked goods to add moisture to breads, cookies, and cakes; slice it into thin coins for vegetable and egg dishes; or spiralize it into noodles. This squash won't dominate the flavor profile and doesn't need to be peeled.

TOMATOES Although technically a fruit, roasted and sun-dried tomatoes provide a grounding umami flavor to satisfy your taste buds' desire for meat and can be added easily to many vegetable and grain dishes.

SWEET POTATOES Add sweet potatoes to puréed soups for a silky texture, or spiralize them into noodles for a quick dinner. Stuff them with black beans, vegetables, and roasted pumpkin seeds for an easy main entrée.

RED BELL PEPPERS Stuff red bell peppers with quinoa for a hearty dinner, or roast some for their savory, tangy flavor. I keep a jar of roasted red peppers in the refrigerator for quick sauces and soups, and to add to casseroles and grain dishes.

Beyond Basics—Give Boredom a Kick

Getting a balanced vegetarian meal is easy, especially with the wide variety of fruits and vegetables typically available year-round. But the key to a non-boring meal are those extra flavor kicks. Flavored olive oils, spices, herbs, a squeeze of citrus, vinegar, hot sauces, and even crunchy breadcrumbs elevate forgettable meals to something you want to make every week. Best of all, they can be added with little fuss. Here are some examples:

BALANCED BASICS	FLAVOR KICK
Corn + black beans + avocado	Season with cumin and lime
Chickpeas + pasta	Toss with briny olives and oregano
Quinoa + Swiss chard + potatoes	Add a dash of smoked paprika or garam masala and a drizzle of olive oil and lemon juice
Butternut squash + apples + quinoa	Go wild with a little cinnamon and cardamom
Chili + cornbread	Top with pickled jalapeño slices and adobo-spiked yogurt
Egg salad + avocado + pita	Spice it up with your favorite hot sauce
Peppers stuffed with quinoa + black beans + corn	Mix in cilantro, lime, and spiced roasted pumpkin seeds
Cauliflower steaks + chickpeas + fried egg	Finish with a dollop of pesto and breadcrumbs

MUSHROOMS The ultimate meaty vegetable, mushrooms can be the main event, as with portabella mushrooms, or chopped and added to traditionally meat-centric dishes, such as meatballs made with chickpeas or lentils.

BABY SPINACH Not as bitter as kale but healthier than iceberg lettuce, spinach is a great compromise green to add to dishes at the last minute for a quick wilt or to layer into a wrap. Romaine lettuce leaves are another great option here.

AVOCADOS They don't last long in the refrigerator, but they don't need to! Their natural creaminess makes you want to eat them right away. They are a great addition to salad dressings and a clever substitute for cream in a chocolate mousse. Their shape, when halved and pitted, makes a perfect bowl to hold egg, bean, or grain salads.

SPAGHETTI SQUASH Once I realized how easy it was to pressure cook this squash in my Instant Pot, it became part of my weekly menu for "pasta." Its mild flavor melds well with most any sauce, green, or vegetable.

BASICS TO BUILD FLAVOR

An early objection from my husband, whom I affectionately refer to as Carnivorous Maximus, was that his dinners would now consist of "horse food." He often punctuated this by stomping one foot, throwing back his head, and neighing. In truth, some of my early meals were probably more fit for horses than humans. It took experimenting and research, but over time, I found a variety of ingredients and techniques to build the kind of flavor we like at our house. Here are some ingredients I always have in my pantry, in addition to ones I make ahead (see Chapter 8: Kitchen Staples, page 167).

Smoke

The smoky-salty flavor of bacon adds depth to dishes, and bacon is one of the meats most missed when moving to a more vegetarian diet. These ingredients help close that gap with a dose of smoke.

- Smoked paprika and its siblings Hungarian hot paprika, Hungarian sweet paprika, and *pimentón ahumado* (a Spanish smoked paprika)
- Chili powder, ancho chile powder, ground cinnamon, ground cardamom, and garam masala, a spice mix often used in Indian dishes
- Dried chipotle chiles for adding to broths, dried beans while they cook, and tomato sauces
- Liquid smoke for broths, soups, and dishes containing tofu, tempeh, and seitan

Broths

Simmering dried beans and soups in flavorful broths can add an extra shot of flavor.

- Dried mushrooms or tomatoes deepen flavors in vegetable broths. (If you make your own broth, first roast the vegetables in the pot.)
- Any of the Better Than Bouillon products, such as Seasoned Vegetable, No Chicken, Mushroom, or No Beef bases, to build flavor in slow cooker meals if you don't pre-sauté vegetables.

Acids

Acids sharpen flavors and are a must for any pantry.

- Lemon and lime juices to make other flavors pop
- Sherry wine vinegar and balsamic vinegar for their magical powers in deepening the flavors of vegetable dishes and providing the perfect accent to earthy beans

Savory-Salty (Umami)

Umami is the fifth taste, and the one that most resembles meat. I highly recommend foods with umami for building this flavor in a dish.

- Mushrooms, either dried or fresh
- Sun-dried tomatoes
- Olives (green, Kalamata, or Niçoise are best)
- Capers
- Parmesan cheese
- Miso paste (both white and red)
- Hoisin sauce

BASICS TO SPEED COOKING

A friend recently told me that her least favorite part of cooking was all the prepping. "Can't I make a good dinner with five minutes of prep or less?" she asked me. Since we're all looking for ideas to make prep easier, here are some items I recommend having in the pantry, refrigerator, and freezer so they're ready for adding to dishes at a moment's notice.

- Canned and frozen beans, and/or zipped plastic bags of beans you've cooked ahead of time and stored in the refrigerator and freezer.
- Bags of frozen, cooked quinoa, farro, or other grains you like to use in dishes.
- Store-bought frozen vegetables, such as cut cauliflower and broccoli, cauliflower rice, corn, sweet potatoes, and peas.
- Frozen garlic cubes, which are available at Trader Joe's and other specialty markets.
- Refrigerated tubes of chili paste, garlic paste, basil, oregano, ginger, and cilantro. They can be squeezed easily into measuring spoons and pots, and they last a long time in the refrigerator. You can find them in the fresh herb area of the produce section of many markets.
- Zipped plastic pouches of refrigerated or frozen pre-sautéed *soffritto*. Soffritto is an Italian term for a mixture of vegetables sautéed in olive oil that creates a foundation of flavor in dishes, similar to France's *mirepoix*. It can be whatever combination of vegetables you like, but usually includes onions, garlic, celery, carrots, and herbs. My favorite version also includes chopped red bell peppers.

VEGETABLE PREP 101

Each recipe in this cookbook requires prepping of at least a few ingredients, although I've tried to keep it as uncomplicated as possible. Prepping takes time, and while it may be meditative to some, for others, it's just the barrier to getting a dish on the table. On any given night, I can relate to either school of thought.

I've already given you my tips to speed up prepping and cooking, and the next section covers my list of kitchen equipment that makes prepping and cooking easier. In this section, I explain a little more about the actual prepping steps referred to in many of the

Storing Fresh Produce and Herbs

Fresh produce and herbs have a limited shelf life, even if we purchase them at a farmers' market hours after they've been harvested. Finding ways to extend their freshness is valuable for both the environment and our wallets. Here are some tips that may help you keep your produce fresher longer.

✗ **Don't** refrigerate tomatoes, eggplant, or potatoes. Cold temperatures change their texture and turn potato starch into sugar more quickly.

✗ **Don't** store fruits such as apricots, apples, avocados, and bananas with vegetables. Fruits often emit ethylene gas, which speeds the spoiling process.

✓ **Do** soak berries for 2 minutes in 5 cups of water and ½ cup of distilled white vinegar. This kills mold spores and promotes a much longer shelf life. Be sure to dry the berries, and line their container with a paper towel before returning them to the refrigerator.

✓ **Do** store herbs in the refrigerator in plastic bags with their stems wrapped in wet paper towels.

✓ **Do** keep basil and mint in a jar on a sunny counter or windowsill. Fill the jar with a few inches of water and cover the basil or mint leaves lightly with plastic.

✓ **Do** chop fresh herbs and place them in an ice cube tray to keep them even longer. Top off the wells in the tray with a neutral oil, freeze, and transfer the cubes to a sealed bag.

recipes. For more information on prepping and cooking various fruits and vegetables, refer to the Reference Guide to Prepping and Cooking Produce on pages 182 to 193.

The types of ingredient prep most often referred to in this cookbook are peeling, trimming, slicing, chopping, dicing, and mincing. Additionally, to make your own cauliflower rice, several recipes include grating. When possible, slice the vegetable in half and, to anchor it, place it cut-side down on your workspace. This makes prepping safer and the vegetable easier to work with.

PEEL I use a Y-shaped peeler for anything long, such as carrots, or anything with a thick skin, such as butternut squash.

TRIM This can refer to removing the bottoms of Brussels sprouts or cauliflower, or the ends of stalks like Swiss chard or asparagus. A paring knife is best for these operations.

COARSE CHOP Vegetables are coarsely chopped when precision is less important. The cut pieces are generally approximately 1-inch square, and it's a good idea to make the pieces similar in size so they'll cook evenly.

CHOP Chopped vegetables are cut into large, equal-size cubes approximately ½-inch square. But here's where it can get confusing: A recipe that includes chopped cauliflower or broccoli requires the florets to be cut into roughly 1-inch pieces. If the pieces are to be cut into smaller pieces, they're generally referred to as finely chopped.

DICE Diced vegetables are cut into cubes roughly half the size of chopped vegetables, or ¼-inch square.

MINCE Minced vegetables are finely sliced into tiny, equal-size pieces that are about ⅛-inch square.

GRATE A box grater is perfect for coarsely shredding raw vegetables, such as beets, carrots, potatoes, or cucumbers, for a slaw. The largest holes are ideal for making cauliflower rice when used on the florets and smaller stalks. A Microplane can be used for shredding smaller vegetables, such as ginger, or for zesting citrus.

Some recipes refer to what I call specialty cuts for ingredients such as corn, bell peppers, leafy greens, and herbs. Those are covered in the Reference Guide to Prepping and Cooking Produce on pages 182 to 193.

Anatomy of a Side Salad

In any given week, I consume meal-worthy salads for lunch and dinner, and you'll find a lot of my favorites in this book. But sometimes, I just want a side salad as an accent to a larger meal, or to pull together a salad for myself that's little more than a snack. Here are some ways I make the often-ignored side salad unforgettable.

HIGHLIGHT A SEASONAL VEGETABLE. Add asparagus in spring, nectarines in summer, apples and pears in fall, and Delicata squash in winter. Get fancy, if you must, with a vegetable peeler to add zucchini or cucumber strips.

GO SUPER-SIMPLE WITH JUST ONE OR TWO INGREDIENTS. Think heirloom tomato slices in varying colors, drizzled with olive oil and a sprinkling of salt and freshly ground pepper. Or toss avocado chunks with slices of plum and a dash of red pepper flakes. Make sure you use a good-quality extra-virgin olive oil. When you don't have a lot of ingredients, the quality of each one can really make an impact on the success of a dish.

USE MORE THAN ONE TYPE OF GREENS. Delicate spring greens mixed with heartier baby spinach is a great combination.

AMP UP BOTH FLAVOR AND TEXTURE. My go-to ingredients for flavor and texture include fresh chopped herbs, nuts, sunflower seeds, or roasted pumpkin seeds.

HAVE A KILLER SALAD DRESSING RECIPE IN YOUR ARSENAL. The quickest way to make a fantastic salad fall flat is to dress it with either an overpowering or boring dressing. I've included some of my favorite dressings in this book, but if I'm on the run, this is the (almost) one-size-fits-all dressing I use.

Lemon Vinaigrette

Makes about ¼ cup / Prep time: 5 minutes

2 tablespoons freshly squeezed lemon juice
½ teaspoon Dijon mustard
1 teaspoon kosher salt
½ teaspoon freshly ground black pepper
¼ cup extra-virgin olive oil

In a small bowl, whisk together the lemon juice, mustard, salt, and pepper. Gradually whisk in the olive oil.

HELPFUL KITCHEN EQUIPMENT

As with anything in life, having the right tools makes a big difference in efficiency. But we only have so much space in our kitchens. No matter the size of my kitchen—and I've had all sizes and shapes through the years—I never have enough room for everything I want. Therefore, any piece of real estate in my kitchen must be earned.

Need to Have

Here is my MVP list of kitchen appliances, all of which you'll find called for in this cookbook's recipes.

- Baking/casserole dishes (2) in different sizes
- Blender (1) for blending soups, puréeing vegetables, and making smoothies
- Box grater (1) for making cauliflower rice
- Cast iron skillet (1) and a heavy-bottomed pot (1) that can be moved from the stove top to the oven with ease. Le Creuset is my go-to brand for heavy-bottomed pots. Their pieces are expensive, but they last forever and come with a lifetime warranty.
- Food processor or mini-processor (1) for fast grating and chopping
- Nonstick skillet (1) for eggs
- Rimmed sheet pans (2) for roasting vegetables and other sheet pan dinners
- Slow cooker or multicooker (1) with both slow cooker and pressure cooker functionality, such as an Instant Pot. Pressure cooking allows you to cook dried beans in a fraction of the time it would take on the stove and speeds up cooking time for notoriously slow-cooking veggies like beets and artichokes.
- Spiralizer (1) for making vegetable noodles, although you can often find pre-spiralized vegetables in the produce department of many grocery stores
- Y-shaped vegetable peeler (1) to easily peel long or tough veggies

Nice to Have

These nice-to-have tools aren't real estate hogs, and I use them often enough to justify owning them.

- Immersion blender (1) for puréeing soups in the pot
- Microplane, rasp-style (1), for zesting citrus and grating fresh ginger
- Small handheld mandoline (1) for quickly slicing a consistent thickness of vegetables for casseroles

If You Don't Have a Slow Cooker or Pressure Cooker

One of the chapters in this cookbook focuses on recipes in either a slow cooker or pressure cooker, or both. If you don't have either piece of equipment but want to try these recipes, they can all be made on your stove top. Here are some guidelines to keep in mind.

CONVERTING SLOW COOKER RECIPES TO THE STOVE TOP

Slow cooker temperatures vary from model to model, making strict adaptation rules difficult. But as a general rule, if a recipe requires anywhere from 6 to 10 hours in a slow cooker using the LOW setting, or 3 to 4 hours using the HIGH setting, it will generally require 45 minutes on the stove top. If a recipe calls for 8 to 10 hours on LOW using the slow cooker, or 4 to 5 hours on HIGH, it will require 50 to 60 minutes on the stove top.

Slow cookers are designed to conserve the liquid from whatever is being cooked and use it for braising the food. When converting a slow cooker recipe to the stove top or oven, which are both much dryer cooking environments, increase the amount of added liquid, sometimes by as much as half, to compensate for evaporation.

CONVERTING PRESSURE COOKER RECIPES TO THE STOVE TOP

When converting a pressure cooker recipe to one cooked on the stove, follow the sauté directions provided to begin the recipe. When the recipe switches to the high pressure function, cover the pot on the stove and cook until done. The time will vary according to what's being cooked, but a good rule of thumb is that most things will take three to four times longer on the stove than in a pressure cooker.

Swap uncooked beans in the recipes for twice as much canned (cooked) beans. For example, if the recipe calls for 1 cup dried beans, you will need 2 cups canned beans, although for soups and stews I always round up so I'm not left with a partial can of beans. If you make this substitution, you will also need to reduce the liquid by 2 cups.

WHAT'S NEXT?

As described earlier in this chapter, this book is divided into chapters that define a type of easy recipe instead of the more traditional outline of types of meals. The vast majority of the recipes can be served for dinner or a hearty lunch, and a few can be breakfast (or breakfast-for-dinner). A handful of the recipes are side dishes that can be easily transformed into meals.

Many of the recipes in the book fall into the lacto-ovo vegetarian group, meaning you will see dairy and eggs in them. A number of recipes include cheese. As a note, many cheeses now use a vegetable rennet as an alternative to animal rennet, so check the label if that's important to you.

Each recipe includes the following dietary labels where applicable:

- dairy-free
- gluten-free
- nut-free
- vegan

I also offer recommendations for adapting the recipes to meet certain diets. And given that I have my own meat eater at the table—and I assume some of you do, too—many of the recipes include tips on which type of meat or fish to add, if you want, and when and how to do it.

Some recipes offer substitution tips, additional ingredient information, and specific prep tips to help you get the most out of every recipe. In Chapter 7 (page 147), which provides recipes for the slow cooker or pressure cooker, every recipe is written for both pieces of equipment. So whether you need something to cook all day while you're at work or need to make it in a jiffy, you'll have the proper directions for cooking it. The pressure cooker recipes for this chapter were tested in a 6-quart Instant Pot Lux Programmable Electric Pressure Cooker. I tested the slow cooker recipes in both an All-Clad 4-Quart

Electric Slow Cooker with Aluminum Insert and an All-Clad 6-Quart Programmable Slow Cooker with Ceramic Insert. Rest assured, the methods for the recipes are written to work with any brand of electric pressure cooker or slow cooker of comparable size.

Finally, a cookbook focused on easy dishes should also be easy to use. Although I've organized the book according to cooking method, I've added a special index on page 194 that's organized into the more traditional type-of-dish categories. This allows you to easily find a list of salads that can be served as a main meal, or a list of pasta dinners if you've got pasta on the brain. I've also included a standard index on page 196 organized by type of ingredient.

If there's a way to sum up my style of cooking as expressed in this book, it's to cook with the seasons and to honor the vegetables and fruits by developing layers of flavor that make them shine. Let's get started!

LEMONY ROMAINE AND
AVOCADO SALAD (PAGE 39)

2

NO COOK

STRAWBERRY-COCONUT SMOOTHIE

Prep time: 10 minutes

A smoothie has great potential to be healthy unless you add sugar in all its various forms. I like to sweeten smoothies with sugar naturally found in fruit, like a very ripe banana. As a banana ages, its starches break down into sugar, but the fruit loses none of its nutritional value. If you feel you need just a little more sweetness, add a bit of honey. **SERVES 1**

Gluten-free • **Nut-free**
Dairy-free and Vegan: Use coconut milk yogurt

1 cup frozen strawberries, slightly thawed

1 very ripe banana, sliced and frozen

½ cup light coconut milk

½ cup plain Greek yogurt

1 teaspoon freshly squeezed lime juice

1 tablespoon chia seeds (optional)

3 or 4 ice cubes

Place all the ingredients in a blender and blend until smooth. If necessary, add additional coconut milk or water to thin the smoothie to your preferred consistency.

SUBSTITUTION TIP: If using fresh strawberries, use 1 cup of ice cubes in the blender in order to achieve a "smoothie" consistency instead of a strawberry-coconut soup.

PER SERVING: CALORIES: 278; TOTAL FAT: 2G; TOTAL CARBS: 57G; FIBER: 9G; SUGAR: 28G; PROTEIN: 14G; SODIUM: 142MG

ALOHA MANGO-PINEAPPLE SMOOTHIE

Prep time: 10 minutes

This smoothie was inspired by one I had many years ago poolside in Hawaii. It was packed with tropical fruit flavors and just a hint of lime. Once I found frozen mango and pineapple chunks in my local market's freezer case, this smoothie was all mine anytime I wanted it. Now I can take a sip, close my eyes, and imagine I'm back in the Aloha State. **SERVES 2**

Gluten-free • **Nut-free**
Dairy-free and Vegan: Use coconut milk yogurt

1 large navel orange, peeled and quartered

1 cup frozen pineapple chunks

1 cup frozen mango chunks

1 tablespoon freshly squeezed lime juice

½ cup plain Greek yogurt

½ cup milk or coconut milk

1 tablespoon chia seeds (optional)

3 or 4 ice cubes

Place all the ingredients in a blender and blend until smooth. If necessary, add additional milk or water to thin the smoothie to your preferred consistency.

INGREDIENT TIP: This healthy smoothie is packed with fiber and vitamin C thanks to the orange, pineapple, and mango.

PER SERVING: CALORIES: 158; TOTAL FAT: 1G; TOTAL CARBS: 35G; FIBER: 5G; SUGAR: 28G; PROTEIN: 7G; SODIUM: 24MG

GAZPACHO

Prep time: 15

Gazpacho's popularity has fostered hundreds of variations featuring ingredients such as watermelon and avocado. But the most important ingredient in any version is the soaked bread, which emulsifies and stabilizes the olive oil to keep it from separating from the soup. The ingredients in this recipe get closer to gazpacho's original Andalusian Spanish roots with a simple combination of tomatoes, white onion, cucumber, and red pepper. Have this for a light lunch, or pour into tiny glasses for an appetizer of soup shots. **SERVES 4**

Dairy-free · Nut-free · Vegan

2 slices white bread

2 pounds ripe, juicy tomatoes, stemmed and quartered

1 white onion, coarsely chopped (about 1½ cups)

1 large cucumber, peeled and coarsely chopped (about 2 cups)

1 red bell pepper, seeded and coarsely chopped

1 teaspoon garlic paste or 2 garlic cloves, finely chopped

½ cup extra-virgin olive oil

3 tablespoons red wine vinegar

1 teaspoon kosher salt

Hot sauce (optional)

1. Soak the bread slices in a bowl of water while you prep the vegetables. Once the bread is thoroughly soaked, remove and gently squeeze out as much water as possible with your hands. Throw away the water, and set the bread aside.

2. Place the tomatoes, onion, cucumber, bell pepper, garlic, olive oil, vinegar, salt, and soaked bread in a blender or food processor fitted with a metal blade. Process until fairly smooth and thickened.

3. Pour into a jar or bowl and chill in the refrigerator for at least 4 hours. The longer it sits, the more the flavors will develop.

4. Stir in hot sauce (if using) before serving.

PREP TIP: If you wish, you can peel the tomatoes before adding them to the blender. For instructions on how to do this, refer to page 192.

GLUTEN-FREE TIP: You can swap out the white bread for a gluten-free variety, but the emulsion may not be as strong without the gluten.

PER SERVING: CALORIES: 336; TOTAL FAT: 26G; TOTAL CARBS: 29G; FIBER: 5G; SUGAR: 10G; PROTEIN: 5G; SODIUM: 848MG

VEGGIE CAESAR WRAPS

Prep time: 15 minutes

Last summer we attended a party to celebrate a friend's milestone birthday. It was a beautiful day for an alfresco meal. A variety of finger foods were arranged on long tablecloth-covered tables in the backyard, where guests gathered to chat with one another. This Caesar wrap was served as a lettuce wrap, and I went back countless times to grab another one. This recipe makes it more of a meal with a tortilla wrap and the addition of croutons. **SERVES 4**

Nut-free
Gluten-free: In place of tortillas, keep the romaine leaves whole for lettuce cups
Dairy-free and Vegan: Use a vegan Caesar salad dressing and omit the Parmesan cheese

2 cups torn romaine lettuce

2 cups diced zucchini

1 cup diced summer squash

½ cup seasoned croutons

¼ cup finely chopped red onion

¼ cup Caesar dressing

4 (8-inch) flour tortillas

2 tablespoons shredded
    Parmesan cheese

1. In a large bowl, combine the romaine, zucchini, summer squash, croutons, and onion. Toss with the Caesar dressing.

2. Lay the tortillas on a flat surface. Spoon 1½ cups of Caesar salad into the middle of each tortilla and sprinkle with the Parmesan cheese. Fold up the bottom edge of each tortilla, then roll up tightly, folding in the sides as you go.

3. Wrap each tortilla in aluminum foil to keep them rolled, or slice in half and skewer with toothpicks.

FLEXITARIAN TIP: Add 1 cup diced chicken or shrimp to the salad, then toss with the dressing. You may need a little extra dressing.

PER SERVING: CALORIES: 263; TOTAL FAT: 12G; TOTAL CARBS: 32G; FIBER: 3G; SUGAR: 3G; PROTEIN: 7G; SODIUM: 662MG

MEDITERRANEAN WRAP WITH SPICY ROASTED CHICKPEAS

Prep time: 10 minutes

This hearty lunch comes together in minutes. Although the recipe calls for homemade versions of hummus and roasted chickpeas, to make the recipe even easier you can purchase your favorite brands at your local market. In place of the chermoula, use a drizzle of olive oil and lemon juice with a pinch of kosher salt and black pepper. **SERVES 1**

Dairy-free · **Nut-free**
Gluten-free and Vegan: Use a romaine lettuce leaf as the wrap

¼ cup Crispy Spicy Chickpeas (page 169) or store-bought

¼ cup halved cherry tomatoes

2 tablespoons quartered Kalamata olives

2 romaine lettuce leaves, torn, or a handful of baby spinach

2 tablespoons Lemony Moroccan Chermoula Sauce (page 172)

¼ cup Smooth and Creamy Hummus (page 176) or store-bought

1 (8-inch) flour tortilla

1. In a medium bowl, combine the chickpeas, tomatoes, olives, and lettuce, and dress with the chermoula.

2. Spread the hummus on the tortilla, leaving a 1-inch border around the edge. Arrange the chickpea mixture on top of the hummus. Fold up the bottom of the tortilla, fold in the sides, and roll up tightly.

INGREDIENT TIP: 1 cup of chickpeas, also known as garbanzo beans, provides nearly 30 percent of your daily protein requirement and offers an extra serving of dietary fiber to help keep blood sugar levels steady.

PER SERVING: CALORIES: 428; TOTAL FAT: 23G; TOTAL CARBS: 47G; FIBER: 9G; SUGAR: 4G; PROTEIN: 13G; SODIUM: 923MG

WHITE BEAN WRAP WITH JALAPEÑO-APPLE SLAW

Prep time: 15 minutes

Consider yourself warned: This may become your go-to slaw. Layer it on your next veggie burger or add it to a pita pocket sandwich for some crunch. It's very versatile and easily absorbs additions, such as sunflower seeds, spicy pumpkins seeds, mandarin orange segments, crushed peanuts, and fresh herbs. Or just keep it simple. You won't go wrong with this on-the-go wrap, no matter how you choose to enjoy it. **SERVES 4**

Dairy-free • **Nut-free**
Gluten-free: Nix the wrap and serve as a salad with slices of mandarin orange

1 large jalapeño pepper, finely chopped

1 medium carrot, peeled and cut into matchsticks

1 Granny Smith apple, cored, and cut into matchsticks

½ cup thinly sliced radishes (3 to 4 radishes)

2 cups finely sliced red cabbage

1 (15-ounce) can white beans, such as navy (pea) beans, drained and rinsed

¼ cup Lime Vinaigrette (page 178)

4 (8-inch) flour tortillas

1. In a large bowl, combine the jalapeño, carrot, apple, radishes, cabbage, and beans. Add the dressing and toss to coat completely.

2. Lay the tortillas on a flat surface and spoon 1½ cups of slaw into the center of each tortilla. Fold up the bottom edge of a tortilla, then roll up tightly, folding in the sides as you go. Repeat with all the wraps. Either wrap each tortilla in aluminum foil to keep them rolled, or slice in half and skewer with toothpicks.

PREP TIP: To enhance the flavors, chill the slaw for one hour in the refrigerator before filling the tortillas.

PER SERVING: CALORIES: 380; TOTAL FAT: 10G; TOTAL CARBS: 63G; FIBER: 9G; SUGAR: 13G; PROTEIN: 14G; SODIUM: 784MG

GREEK PITA POCKETS

Prep time: 15 minutes

This is a classic Greek salad in the form of a pita sandwich, but feel free to dispatch with the bread and take the salad to work in a large Mason jar. Whisk up the vinaigrette and pour it into the bottom of the jar. Then, layer the salad ingredients in the following order: beans, onion, cheese, olives, tomatoes, cucumber, and end with the spinach leaves. This keeps the heartier crunchy vegetables at the bottom, and the more tender veggies at the top. Screw the top on tightly and pour everything into a bowl at work when you're ready to eat. **MAKES 2 PITAS**

Nut-free

1 (15-ounce) can black beans, drained and rinsed

½ cup quartered cherry tomatoes

¼ cup diced cucumber

¼ cup crumbled feta cheese

2 tablespoons halved Kalamata olives

2 tablespoons finely chopped red onion

1 cup baby spinach leaves

3 tablespoons Lemon Vinaigrette (page 15)

1 pita

1. In a medium bowl, place the beans, tomatoes, cucumber, cheese, olives, onion, and spinach. Toss with the vinaigrette.

2. Slice the pita round in half, split open, and stuff with the salad.

FLEXITARIAN TIP: Add slices of flank steak or lamb to the salad.

PER SERVING (½ PITA): CALORIES: 494; TOTAL FAT: 14G; TOTAL CARBS: 71G; FIBER: 19G; SUGAR: 7G; PROTEIN: 22G; SODIUM: 1004MG

CAULIFLOWER RICE TABBOULEH

Prep time: 20 minutes

Tabbouleh is a Middle Eastern dish frequently made with bulgur, tomatoes, cucumber, onion, and finely chopped parsley and mint. It's typically served as a *mezze* (appetizer) with pita bread and lettuce for making small wraps or handheld boats. In this version, cauliflower rice is a low-carb substitute for the bulgur. Cauliflower rice is popular enough to be found in the produce and frozen food sections of most markets, and it can be eaten either raw, steamed, roasted, or lightly sautéed in oil. **MAKES 8 CUPS**

Dairy-free • **Gluten-free** • **Nut-free** • **Vegan**

---

4 cups cauliflower rice

1½ cups cherry tomatoes, quartered

1 cup chopped fresh parsley

1 cup chopped fresh mint

1 cup thinly sliced snap peas

1 small cucumber, cut into ¼-inch pieces (about 1 cup)

¼ cup thinly sliced scallions, white and light green parts only

3 to 4 tablespoons freshly squeezed lemon juice

3 to 4 tablespoons extra-virgin olive oil

1 teaspoon kosher salt

½ teaspoon freshly ground black pepper

1. In a large bowl, combine the cauliflower rice, tomatoes, parsley, mint, snap peas, cucumber, and scallions, and lightly toss.

2. Add the lemon juice and olive oil, and toss again. Season with the salt and pepper to your liking.

PREP TIP: If you can't find premade cauliflower rice in your market, make your own! Simply remove the florets from ½ head of cauliflower and grate them on the large holes of a box grater. Alternatively, use the grater attachment for your food processor, or a mini-processor.

LEFTOVER TIP: This dish is even more flavorful the next day, and it retains all of the cauliflower's crunchiness. However, by the third day, the herbs will lose their freshness.

PER SERVING (2 CUPS): CALORIES: 220; TOTAL FAT: 15G; TOTAL CARBS: 20G; FIBER: 8G; SUGAR: 8G; PROTEIN: 7G; SODIUM: 627MG

MEXICAN TACO BOWL

Prep time: 15 minutes

Beans take on the flavors of almost anything they're mixed with. In this simple salad, which is filling enough to be dinner, they take center stage with a cast of ingredients that may already be in your refrigerator. Feel free to roast your own peppers, but chopping up a few from a jar practically guarantees dinner will be ready in less than 15 minutes. **SERVES 4**

Gluten-free • **Nut-free**
Dairy-free and Vegan: Eliminate the cheese or use vegan mozzarella

2 (15-ounce) cans pinto beans, drained and rinsed, or 3 cups cooked pinto beans

1 cup halved cherry tomatoes

1 cup chopped roasted red bell peppers

1 ear corn, kernels sliced off the cob (about 1 cup)

½ avocado, chopped

½ cup sliced scallions, white and light green parts only

½ cup crumbled Cotija cheese or other mild cheese

1 cup chopped baby romaine lettuce

¼ cup Lime Vinaigrette (page 178)

1 cup crumbled corn tortilla chips

1. In a large bowl, combine the beans, tomatoes, peppers, corn, avocado, scallions, cheese, and lettuce.

2. Add half of the vinaigrette and toss. Add additional dressing as desired, and finish with a topping of tortilla chips.

PER SERVING: CALORIES: 439; TOTAL FAT: 19G; TOTAL CARBS: 57G; FIBER: 16G; SUGAR: 9G; PROTEIN: 18G; SODIUM: 442MG

How to Cook a Perfect Pot of Beans

I've cooked beans on the stove, in the slow cooker, and in an electric pressure cooker, and I heartily recommend either of the latter two choices if you have the equipment. But there are a couple of considerations before you get cooking.

For a slow cooker

Place 1 cup of dried beans, 4 cups of vegetable broth, ½ teaspoon of kosher salt, ½ onion, and a dried chipotle chile in the cooker. Cover and cook for 3 to 4 hours on high or 6 to 8 hours on low. Discard the onion and pepper. Drain, but retain the liquid for use in recipes calling for vegetable broth.

For an electric pressure cooker

Place 1 cup of dried beans, 4 cups of vegetable broth, ½ teaspoon of kosher salt, ½ onion, and a dried chipotle chile in the inner cooking pot. Set the pressure cooking time to 40 minutes at high pressure. When cooking finishes, quick release the pressure.

TO SALT OR NOT TO SALT: After many years of judiciously not salting before cooking, I'm firmly in the pre-salting camp. I use ½ teaspoon of kosher salt for every cup of dried beans.

TO SOAK OR NOT TO SOAK: Any bean, except fast-cooking lentils, benefits from an overnight soak, but I rarely remember to do this. If you have hard water, though, or are cooking older beans, an overnight soak in water with ¼ teaspoon of baking soda can help tenderize the beans.

MASON JAR EDAMAME SALAD

Prep time: 15 minutes

Mason jar salads are ideal when you need to eat lunch at your desk and want something easy, portable, and completely satisfying. I've also piled this salad into a plastic container to take with me on long weekend hikes. This recipe gets bonus points because you can make it the night before. If you make it ahead, leave the basil and mint out until the next morning. **SERVES 1**

Dairy-free · **Gluten-free** · **Nut-free** · **Vegan**

1 cup edamame beans, shelled, or thawed frozen

1 cup fresh corn kernels

¼ cup chopped red onion

1 red bell pepper, chopped

2 to 3 tablespoons freshly squeezed lime juice

5 or 6 fresh basil leaves, sliced into thin slivers

5 or 6 fresh mint leaves, sliced into thin slivers

Kosher salt, to taste

Freshly ground black pepper, to taste

1. In a large Mason jar, place all of the ingredients, and don't worry about layering.

2. Seal the jar tightly and shake it up. Eat right from the jar or pour into a bowl for lunch.

PER SERVING: CALORIES: 299; TOTAL FAT: 9G; TOTAL CARBS: 38G; FIBER: 12G; SUGAR: 13G; PROTEIN: 20G; SODIUM: 165MG

FRUITY BROCCOLI AND BEAN SALAD

Prep time: 15 minutes

I like crunch in my salads and typically make this one with raw broccoli. But the broccoli spears can also be tossed with a little olive oil and lemon and roasted for 20 minutes in a preheated 450°F oven. Just let them cool a bit before combining them with the other ingredients. This classic salad works well as a main dish or a side and completely changes its personality if you switch up the dressing from a miso-spiked tahini to ranch, blue cheese, or a simple vinaigrette. **SERVES 4**

Dairy-free • **Gluten-free**
Nut-free: Omit the peanuts
Vegan: Use ranch, blue cheese, or a yogurt-based dressing

4½ cups thinly sliced broccoli florets and stems

1 (15-ounce) can white beans, drained and rinsed

2 large celery stalks, thinly sliced

¾ cup halved red grapes

⅓ cup smashed roasted and salted peanuts

¼ cup diced red onion

½ cup Tahini Miso Dressing (page 179) or store-bought tahini dressing

1. In a large bowl, combine the broccoli, beans, celery, grapes, peanuts, and onion.

2. Pour the dressing over the salad and toss to coat the ingredients. Add more dressing, if needed.

FLEXITARIAN TIP: Add 1 cup of roasted chicken chunks to the salad.

PER SERVING: CALORIES: 336; TOTAL FAT: 13G; TOTAL CARBS: 45G; FIBER: 15G; SUGAR: 10G; PROTEIN: 16G; SODIUM: 349MG

MEXICAN STREET CORN SALAD

Prep time: 15 minutes

If you've never had Mexican street corn, you've been missing out. Street vendors all over Mexico City grill ears of corn and roll them in a mayonnaise-based sauce mixed with cotija cheese, red onion, jalapeño, lime, and chili spices. This salad is an uncooked version of that treat. For a variation on an already delicious salad, you can grill the corn before removing the kernels from the cobs. **SERVES 4**

Gluten-free • Nut-free

FOR THE DRESSING

8 ounces cotija cheese, crumbled

¼ cup mayonnaise

½ jalapeño pepper, diced

3 garlic cloves, minced, or 1 teaspoon garlic paste

2 tablespoons freshly squeezed lime juice

¾ teaspoon kosher salt

½ teaspoon chili powder

FOR THE SALAD

4 ears corn, kernels sliced off the cob, or 4 cups frozen corn kernels, thawed

1 pint cherry tomatoes, halved

½ cup chopped red onion

½ cup chopped basil leaves

1. To make the dressing, combine the cheese, mayonnaise, jalapeño, garlic, lime juice, salt, and chili powder together in a small bowl.

2. To make the salad, combine the corn, tomatoes, onion, and basil leaves in a large bowl. Add the dressing one spoonful at a time, and toss until the salad is well coated.

SERVING TIP: This salad is perfect on its own but can be made heartier by adding 1 (15-ounce) can of (drained and rinsed) pinto or black beans. It can also be used as a topping for tacos and pita pocket sandwiches, or mixed with additional dressing and served as a dip with tortilla chips.

FLEXITARIAN TIP: Add crumbled bacon to the salad.

PER SERVING: CALORIES: 416; TOTAL FAT: 25G; TOTAL CARBS: 35G; FIBER: 5G; SUGAR: 8G; PROTEIN: 19G; SODIUM: 905MG

SUMMER ZOODLE SALAD WITH BASIL AND MOZZARELLA

Prep time: 15 minutes, plus 30 minutes to marinate

Zucchini noodles, or zoodles, started the low-carb vegetable noodle craze, and it was pure genius. Use a potato peeler, julienne peeler, mandoline, or spiralizer to make noodles from zucchini and use in place of traditional wheat pasta. Zoodles can be eaten raw, as in this salad, added to a soup, steamed, or lightly sautéed in olive oil. They've become so popular, I can even find zucchini noodles tucked into cartons in the produce section of my market, alongside noodles made from butternut squash and sweet potatoes. **SERVES 4**

Gluten-free • Nut-free
Dairy-free and Vegan: Use vegan mozzarella

1 pound ripe tomatoes, diced, with their juices

2 peaches or nectarines, diced, with their juices

¼ cup fresh basil, thinly sliced

1 teaspoon garlic paste or 2 garlic cloves, minced

2 tablespoons capers, coarsely chopped

½ teaspoon kosher salt, plus more for seasoning

½ teaspoon freshly ground black pepper, plus more for seasoning

½ teaspoon sugar

4 cups zucchini noodles

½ cup grated mozzarella cheese

Extra-virgin olive oil, for drizzling

1. In a large bowl, combine the tomatoes, peaches, basil, garlic, capers, salt, pepper, and sugar. Let sit at room temperature for 30 minutes to soften, and allow the flavors to meld together.

2. Toss with the zucchini noodles and top with mozzarella. Season with salt and pepper to taste, and finish with a drizzle of olive oil.

VARIATION TIP: Sauté the zoodles for 5 minutes in 1 tablespoon of olive oil before topping them with the tomatoes and peaches.

PER SERVING: CALORIES: 97; TOTAL FAT: 2G; TOTAL CARBS: 20G; FIBER: 5G; SUGAR: 14G; PROTEIN: 5G; SODIUM: 495MG

SHAVED BRUSSELS SPROUT SALAD

Prep time: 15 minutes

Brussels sprouts are a divisive vegetable, but this salad can be a game changer with its crunch of walnuts and flavors of lemon and mustard. The biggest decision is how to accomplish shaving the sprouts. My weapon of choice is a food processor fitted with the grater blade. I just pop a few sprouts at a time down the shoot and, presto, they're grated in seconds. **SERVES 4**

Gluten-free
Dairy-free and Vegan: Swap the cheese and honey for vegan mozzarella and agave nectar

---

1 pound Brussels sprouts

½ cup walnuts,
    coarsely chopped

½ cup grated Parmesan
    cheese, divided

2 tablespoons dried cranberries
    or dried cherries

2 tablespoons freshly squeezed
    lemon juice

1 teaspoon honey

2 teaspoons whole-
    grain mustard

Pinch kosher salt

Pinch freshly ground
    black pepper

¼ cup extra-virgin olive oil

1. Trim the stubby ends of the Brussels sprouts using a sharp knife, then slice the sprouts into thin shavings. You can do this by hand or with a mandoline, but a food processor fitted with a grater blade makes quick work of the sprouts.

2. In a large bowl, toss the shaved Brussels sprouts with the walnuts, ¼ cup of Parmesan cheese, and the dried cranberries.

3. In a small bowl, whisk together the lemon juice, honey, mustard, salt, pepper, and olive oil. Drizzle half of the dressing on the salad, and toss to combine. Add the remaining dressing as desired, and correct for seasoning.

4. Top with the remaining ¼ cup of Parmesan.

FLEXITARIAN TIP: Add crumbled bacon to the salad.

PER SERVING: CALORIES: 333; TOTAL FAT: 26G; TOTAL CARBS: 20G; FIBER: 6G; SUGAR: 9G; PROTEIN: 11G; SODIUM: 221MG

LEBANESE CHOPPED SALAD

Prep time: 15 minutes

This salad is known by many names—fattoush, Arab salad, Israeli salad, and chopped salad—and is popular throughout the Middle East. It's typically made with torn pieces of toasted or stale pita, tomatoes, cucumbers, radishes, and often some greens. This salad can be simply dressed in olive oil and lemon juice, but the buttermilk dressing adds just the right touch of tart. Feel free to substitute a store-bought buttermilk dressing. **SERVES 4**

Nut-free

FOR THE SALAD

1 (15-ounce) can chickpeas, drained and rinsed

1 cup halved cherry tomatoes

1 small cucumber, diced

2 scallions, thinly sliced

½ cup crumbled feta cheese

¼ cup chopped fresh mint

¼ cup chopped fresh parsley

2 pita rounds or other flatbread, torn into pieces

FOR THE DRESSING

½ cup buttermilk

2 tablespoons extra-virgin olive oil

2 tablespoons freshly squeezed lemon juice

1 teaspoon garlic paste or 2 garlic cloves, minced

½ teaspoon ground cumin

¼ teaspoon kosher salt

1. To make the salad, combine the chickpeas, tomatoes, cucumber, scallions, feta, mint, parsley, and pita in a large bowl.

2. To make the dressing, whisk together the buttermilk, olive oil, lemon juice, garlic, cumin, and salt in a small bowl.

3. Before serving, pour the dressing over the salad ingredients and toss until well coated.

PER SERVING: CALORIES: 417; TOTAL FAT: 18G; TOTAL CARBS: 49G; FIBER: 9G; SUGAR: 9G; PROTEIN: 18G; SODIUM: 405MG

SOUTHWEST LAYERED SALAD

Prep time: 20 minutes

This salad was inspired by my favorite seven-layer Mexican dip. I first had it while visiting a friend many years ago, and was instantly smitten by the combination of refried beans, sour cream with taco seasonings, guacamole, tomatoes, and cheese. This salad is gorgeous layered in a glass bowl, and can then be dressed and tossed at the table. It can be made ahead and refrigerated, but don't add the taco chips and dressing until ready to serve. **SERVES 4**

Gluten-free • Nut-free

1 (15-ounce) can black or pinto beans, rinsed and drained

¼ cup salsa

3 cups romaine lettuce, chopped

2 cups fresh corn kernels

1 cup halved cherry tomatoes

1 orange, yellow, or red bell pepper, diced

½ cup queso fresco, crumbled, or shredded Cheddar cheese

1 avocado, diced

1 cup crumbled tortilla chips

¼ cup ranch dressing

1 tablespoon barbecue sauce or taco seasoning

1. In a small bowl, stir together the black beans and salsa. Spread across the bottom of a large serving bowl.

2. Layer the following ingredients in the serving bowl in this order: lettuce, corn, tomatoes, bell pepper, cheese, avocado, and tortilla chips.

3. In a small bowl, whisk together the ranch dressing and barbecue sauce, and serve on the side.

FLEXITARIAN TIP: Add crumbled bacon or diced roasted chicken as an additional layer between the tomatoes and the bell pepper for extra protein and a nice color contrast.

PER SERVING: CALORIES: 460; TOTAL FAT: 23G; TOTAL CARBS: 52G; FIBER: 15G; SUGAR: 8G; PROTEIN: 16G; SODIUM: 376MG

LEMONY ROMAINE AND AVOCADO SALAD

Prep time: 15 minutes

This is my go-to side salad, although I eliminate the pomegranate seeds when I can't find them outside of the late-fall and winter months. It's extremely flexible, as all side salads should be. Sometimes I use Bibb lettuce mixed with the romaine. Other times I turn it into a main salad by adding cauliflower or broccoli florets, or slices of beets and a dollop of goat cheese. Any way you make it, it's a great little salad to have in your arsenal. **SERVES 6**

Gluten-free • Nut-free • Vegan

1 head romaine lettuce

½ cup pomegranate seeds

¼ cup pine nuts

¼ cup Lemon Vinaigrette (page 15)

2 avocados

Freshly ground black pepper

1. Remove and discard any wilted leaves from the romaine. Wash and spin-dry the remaining leaves. Tear or slice the leaves into bite-size pieces. Place the leaves in a large bowl, and toss with the pomegranate seeds, pine nuts, and half of the vinaigrette.

2. Slice the avocados in half. Remove the pit from each, and slice the avocados into long thin slices. Using a large spoon, carefully scoop the slices out of the peel.

3. Layer the avocado slices on top of the lettuce in the bowl, and drizzle half of the remaining dressing over them. Carefully toss using your hands or a large metal spoon. Add the remaining dressing as needed.

4. Finish with a few sprinkles of pepper.

PER SERVING: CALORIES: 217; TOTAL FAT: 20G; TOTAL CARBS: 11G; FIBER: 6G; SUGAR: 4G; PROTEIN 3G; SODIUM: 406MG

BOK CHOY–ASPARAGUS SALAD

Prep time: 20 minutes

Bok choy is most often cooked, showing up in many Asian-influenced soups and braised dishes. But this nutritious green is just as good raw, adding great crunch to salads. Considered one of the most nutrient-dense foods in the world, bok choy is packed with vitamins, folate, antioxidants, and calcium, so whether you eat it cooked or raw, make sure you pick some up the next time you head to the market. **SERVES 4**

Dairy-free · **Gluten-free** · **Nut-free** · **Vegan**

4 cups coarsely chopped baby bok choy

1½ cups asparagus, trimmed and cut into 1½-inch lengths

1 cup cauliflower rice

1 cup strawberries, chopped into bite-size chunks

1 mango, peeled and diced

½ cup scallions, sliced into 1-inch lengths

¼ cup Lemon Vinaigrette (page 15)

In a large bowl, combine the bok choy, asparagus, cauliflower rice, strawberries, mango, and scallions. Drizzle with the vinaigrette and gently toss.

FLEXITARIAN TIP: Add cooked shrimp to the salad.

PER SERVING: CALORIES: 210; TOTAL FAT: 14G; TOTAL CARBS: 21G; FIBER: 5G; SUGAR: 16G; PROTEIN: 3G; SODIUM: 637MG

CAULIFLOWER, KALE, AND APPLE SALAD

Prep time: 25 minutes

Cauliflower and apples are perfect foils for each other—a natural pairing—and many different kinds of apples work well in this recipe. Any crispy, sweet apple will do the trick, whether it's a Fuji, Honeycrisp, or Pink Lady. Granny Smith apples are a little too tart for this salad. **SERVES 4**

Dairy-free • Gluten-free • Nut-free • Vegan

3 cups chopped
   cauliflower florets

2 cups baby kale

1 crisp, sweet apple, cored
   and chopped

¼ cup chopped fresh basil

¼ cup chopped fresh
   Italian parsley

¼ cup chopped fresh mint

⅓ cup thinly sliced scallions

2 tablespoons yellow raisins

1 tablespoon chopped sun-dried
   tomatoes

½ cup Tahini Miso Dressing
   (page 179)

¼ cup Roasted Pumpkin Seeds
   (page 170)

In a large bowl, combine the cauliflower, kale, apple, basil, parsley, mint, scallions, raisins, and tomatoes. Toss with the dressing and serve with a sprinkling of pumpkin seeds.

PREP TIP: Smaller cauliflower florets can be left whole, but chop any large ones into smaller florets.

FLEXITARIAN TIP: Add roasted chicken or crispy bacon crumbles to the salad.

PER SERVING: CALORIES: 198; TOTAL FAT: 8G; TOTAL CARBS: 32G; FIBER: 7G; SUGAR: 16G; PROTEIN: 7G; SODIUM: 349MG

BUTTERNUT SQUASH SOUP
WITH APPLE CIDER (PAGE 64)

3
THIRTY MINUTES MAX

PORTABELLA EGGS FLORENTINE

Prep time: 5 minutes • **Cook time:** 25 minutes

Portabellas are actually cremini mushrooms all grown up. The name *portabella* came onto the scene in the 1980s as a way to glamorize cremini harvested too late. It worked. In fact, portabellas are so popular today, some cremini are marketed as "baby bella" mushrooms. Because they're older, portabellas are a little drier, with a more pronounced mushroom flavor. Their size provides a lot of vegetarian entrée opportunities. You'll also see them referred to as portobello, portabello, and portobella mushrooms. The Mushroom Council, however, has tried to standardize the spelling as portabella. **SERVES 2**

Gluten-free • Nut-free

2 large portabella mushroom caps

2 tablespoons balsamic vinegar

1 tablespoon olive oil

½ teaspoon kosher salt, divided

½ teaspoon freshly ground black pepper, divided

1 tablespoon unsalted butter

1 teaspoon garlic paste

½ teaspoon Dijon mustard

3 tablespoons heavy (whipping) cream

1 (5-ounce) bag baby spinach

2 large eggs

1. Preheat the oven to 400°F.

2. Remove the stems from the portabellas and scrape out the gills with a spoon.

3. In a medium-size bowl, whisk together the vinegar, olive oil, and ¼ teaspoon each of salt and pepper. Add the portabellas and coat them with the marinade.

4. Place the mushrooms in an oven-safe skillet, gill-side up, and roast for 15 minutes.

5. While the portabellas are roasting, melt the butter in a medium skillet over medium heat. Stir in the garlic paste, mustard, and remaining ¼ teaspoon each of salt and pepper. Cook for about 1 minute. Whisk in the cream and cook until thickened, about 1 minute. Fold in the spinach and gently toss until completely coated and wilted, 2 to 3 minutes.

6. Once the portabellas have roasted for 15 minutes, spoon the creamed spinach into their cavities. Form a nest within the creamed spinach using a large spoon. Break an egg into each nest. It's fine if the white of the egg runs over a bit as long as the yolk remains inside the mushroom cap. Roast for another 10 to 12 minutes, or until the egg white is completely set but the yolk remains runny.

PER SERVING: CALORIES: 306; TOTAL FAT: 27G; TOTAL CARBS: 9G; FIBER: 3G; SUGAR: 2G; PROTEIN: 11G; SODIUM: 777MG

QUINOA AND NECTARINE SLAW

Prep time: 10 minutes • **Cook time:** 6 minutes

This simple salad is a light and refreshing meal on a hot summer day. The nectarines should be at, or close to, their peak ripeness so that their natural sweetness can perfectly combine with the earthy pumpkin seeds. If you don't see ripe nectarines at your market, you can use peaches, since nectarines are just peaches without the fuzz. **SERVES 2**

Gluten-free • **Nut-free**
Dairy-free and Vegan: Omit the feta

1 cup cooked quinoa, at room temperature (see page 55)

2 nectarines, cut into ½-inch wedges

½ cup shredded white cabbage

½ cup chopped curly kale

⅓ cup thinly sliced scallions

⅓ cup Roasted Pumpkin Seeds (page 170)

3 tablespoons Lemon Vinaigrette (page 15)

½ cup feta cheese (optional)

1. In a large bowl, combine the quinoa, nectarines, cabbage, kale, scallions, and pumpkin seeds. Toss with the vinaigrette.

2. Serve topped with the feta cheese (if using).

PER SERVING: CALORIES: 396; TOTAL FAT: 18G; TOTAL CARBS: 52G; FIBER: 7G; SUGAR: 12G; PROTEIN: 11G; SODIUM: 607MG

ZUCCHINI FRITTERS

Prep time: 15 minutes • **Cook time:** 15 minutes

The secret to these fritters is to hold off flipping them until they get a crispy crust. It doesn't take long, but if you don't wait, these tender patties may fall apart when flipped. These are perfect for both a brunch and a light dinner with a salad. I've also made them for a party appetizer. I form small patties with 2 tablespoons of the mixture, then sauté them for a couple of minutes on each side in a little olive oil, and serve with a dollop of a creamy dip or dressing. **MAKES 10 FRITTERS**

Nut-free

1 Yukon Gold potato

½ cup cooked quinoa (see page 55)

1 large zucchini, grated using the large holes on a box grater

1 cup freshly crumbled feta cheese

½ cup thinly sliced leek, white and light green parts only

¼ cup panko breadcrumbs

1 egg, beaten

1 teaspoon freshly squeezed lemon juice

1 teaspoon kosher salt

½ teaspoon freshly ground black pepper

2 tablespoons olive oil

1. Poke a few holes in the potato. Microwave on high until tender, about 5 minutes. When cool enough to handle, peel and coarsely grate into a large bowl. You should end up with about 1 cup of grated potato.

2. Place the potato, quinoa, zucchini, cheese, leek, breadcrumbs, egg, lemon juice, salt, and pepper in a large bowl. Toss a few times to thoroughly mix.

3. Scoop out ¼ cup of the zucchini batter and form it into a patty. Repeat with the remaining batter.

4. Heat the olive oil in a large skillet over medium heat. Add the zucchini patties and cook for about 4 minutes, or until browned and slightly crisp. Carefully flip the fritters over and continue cooking for another 3 to 4 minutes.

5. Serve warm with a salad.

MAKE IT AHEAD: The fritters can be made ahead through step 4, then wrapped in plastic and refrigerated for a couple of days before being cooked.

PER SERVING (2 FRITTERS): CALORIES: 235; TOTAL FAT: 14G; TOTAL CARBS: 20G; FIBER: 3G; SUGAR: 3G; PROTEIN: 9G; SODIUM: 863MG

LOADED SWEET POTATO NACHO FRIES

Prep time: 15 minutes • **Cook time:** 15 minutes

This nacho dish is a perfect appetizer for a party—think Super Bowl party—or a fun meal with your family. It's very flexible, so go ahead and swap in the vegetables you and your family prefer. You can make your own sweet potato fries instead of using the frozen variety, but they'll take a little longer to slice up and bake. Frozen fries can be cooked on the stove or baked in the oven. The oven will take a little longer, but you'll avoid any splattering of oil. **SERVES 2**

Nut-free

2 tablespoons olive oil

½ (19-ounce) bag frozen sweet potato fries

¼ teaspoon kosher salt, plus ⅛ teaspoon

¼ teaspoon ground cumin

1 (15-ounce) can black beans, drained and rinsed

1 cup halved cherry tomatoes

1 cup fresh or frozen corn kernels

2 scallions, thinly sliced

½ cup grated Mexican cheeses or Cheddar cheese

½ cup Mexican crema or sour cream

¼ cup plain Greek yogurt

1 whole chipotle chile in adobo sauce, minced into a paste

1 tablespoon freshly squeezed lime juice

1 avocado, chopped

1. Heat the oil in a cast iron skillet or other heavy skillet over medium-high heat. Add the sweet potato fries, and season with ¼ teaspoon of salt and the cumin. Sauté for about 10 minutes, stirring occasionally to prevent overbrowning. If there's a lot of splattering from ice crystals, reduce the heat and cover with a lid.

2. When the fries are tender, toss one final time, then top with the beans, tomatoes, corn, scallions, and cheese. Cover with a lid and cook for 2 to 3 minutes, or until the cheese is melted.

3. In a small bowl, make a chipotle crema by combining the Mexican crema, yogurt, chipotle chile paste, lime juice, and remaining ⅛ teaspoon of salt.

4. Serve the nachos topped with avocado chunks and drizzled with the chipotle crema.

FLEXITARIAN TIP: Fry ½ pound chorizo in a separate pan. Drain and add to the sweet potato fries with the black beans in step 2.

SUBSTITUTION TIP: Use ranch dressing as a quick and easy substitution for the chipotle crema.

PER SERVING: CALORIES: 724; TOTAL FAT: 45G; TOTAL CARBS: 66G; FIBER: 24G; SUGAR: 3G; PROTEIN: 26G; SODIUM: 793MG

SMASHED CHICKPEA AVOCADO TOASTS

Prep time: 15 minutes

The chickpea spread portion of this recipe is great for making ahead. It comes together in no time and will last a few days in the refrigerator. You may not normally have fresh dill in your refrigerator, but don't be tempted to skip it. It's worth a trip to the market, as it completely transforms this dish. This recipe calls for seasoned salt (and I use Jane's Krazy Mixed-Up Salt), but if you don't have any, just use coarse sea salt and freshly ground pepper as a finishing touch. **SERVES 4**

Dairy-free · **Nut-free**
Gluten-free: Serve in a lettuce wrap
Vegan: Use vegan mayonnaise

1 (15-ounce) can chickpeas, drained and rinsed

½ cup finely diced celery

¼ cup thinly sliced scallions, white parts and most of the green stalk

2 tablespoons mayonnaise

1½ tablespoons minced garlic or garlic paste

1 tablespoon chopped fresh dill

2 teaspoons freshly squeezed lemon juice

½ teaspoon kosher salt

4 slices whole-wheat bread

2 avocados, sliced lengthwise

4 tablespoons extra-virgin olive oil

Seasoned salt, to taste

1. Place the chickpeas in a shallow bowl and coarsely smash them with a fork or potato masher. They shouldn't be completely smooth or completely whole.

2. Stir in the celery, scallions, mayonnaise, garlic, dill, lemon juice, and salt to create a spread.

3. Toast the bread. Spread 3 to 4 tablespoons of the chickpea mixture on top of each piece of toast. Arrange a couple of slices of avocado on the chickpea spread, and finish with a drizzle of olive oil and a shower of seasoned salt.

PER SERVING: CALORIES: 565; TOTAL FAT: 39G; TOTAL CARBS: 46G; FIBER: 15G; SUGAR: 7G; PROTEIN: 13G; SODIUM: 501MG

BROCCOLI AND WHITE BEANS ON TOAST

Prep time: 10 minutes • **Cook time:** 20 minutes

Through the years, I've tried a plethora of ways to speed up garlic prep. I've purchased countless gizmos to remove the skins more quickly, and have worked with various mincing, smashing, and grinding techniques. Nothing has served me as well as just buying garlic paste. I use it almost every day. Garlic is good for you, too. It can help fight the common cold, reduce blood pressure, and improve cholesterol levels. It has antioxidants to fight dementia and can detoxify heavy metals in your body. **MAKES 6 TOASTS**

Dairy-free • **Nut-free** • **Vegan**

2 pounds broccoli, stalks and florets, trimmed, peeled, and chopped into ½-inch pieces

3 tablespoons olive oil, divided

1 teaspoon kosher salt, divided

2 teaspoons garlic paste or minced garlic

2 teaspoons minced fresh rosemary or ½ to ¾ teaspoon dried rosemary

¼ teaspoon freshly ground black pepper

2 (15-ounce) cans cannellini beans, drained and rinsed

6 slices crusty bread, such as ciabatta

½ cup Balsamic Roasted Tomatoes (page 168)

1. Preheat the oven to 425°F. Line a rimmed baking sheet with parchment paper.

2. Toss the broccoli with 2 tablespoons of olive oil and ½ teaspoon of salt. Arrange on the baking sheet in a single layer and roast until crisp-tender, 15 to 20 minutes.

3. While the broccoli is roasting, heat the remaining 1 tablespoon of olive oil in a medium skillet over medium heat. Add the garlic, rosemary, and pepper and sauté until fragrant, about 1 minute. Add the beans and cook, tossing occasionally, for 10 minutes. The beans should be very soft.

4. Transfer the bean mixture to a large bowl. Smash with a fork until you have a chunky spread.

5. Toast the bread.

6. Spread the mashed beans on the toasts, and top with the roasted broccoli and tomatoes. Serve the toasts warm and eat with a knife and fork.

SUBSTITUTION TIP: If you don't have the Balsamic Roasted Tomatoes on hand, halve cherry tomatoes, toss in olive oil, and arrange, cut-side up, on another part of the baking sheet with the broccoli in step 1. Roast them with the broccoli, but take them out of the oven after 10 minutes, then drizzle with 1 teaspoon of balsamic vinegar.

PER SERVING: CALORIES: 268; TOTAL FAT: 9G; TOTAL CARBS: 39G; FIBER: 10G; SUGAR: 3G; PROTEIN: 13G; SODIUM: 557MG

ASPARAGUS, LEEK, AND RICOTTA FLATBREADS

Prep time: 10 minutes · **Sauté time:** 10 minutes · **Cook time:** 10 minutes

Flatbreads have been around since early Egyptian times but are popping up today on trendy menus all over the country. Flatbread is unleavened bread made with flour, water, and salt, and either baked or cooked on a hot griddle. Every ancient civilization has one, from tortillas, pizza, pita, naan, and roti to lavash, frybread, piadina, chapati, bhakri, puri, arepa, and matzo. In many cultures making flatbreads is an art. They can be rolled into a sandwich, cupped in your hands to hold a curry, or toasted flat for a sturdy foundation, like in this recipe. **SERVES 2**

Nut-free

2 large eggs

2 slices naan or other thick flatbread, such as pizza crust

2 tablespoons olive oil, divided

1 teaspoon kosher salt, divided

½ teaspoon freshly ground black pepper, divided

2 medium leeks, white and light green parts only, thinly sliced crosswise

1 bundle asparagus, about ½ pound when trimmed, cut into ½-inch pieces

1 teaspoon dried thyme or 2½ teaspoons chopped fresh thyme

4 tablespoons Lemon Vinaigrette (page 15), divided

⅓ cup part-skim ricotta cheese

4 teaspoons Parmesan cheese

1. Preheat the oven to 400°F.

2. In a small pot, cover the eggs with 2 inches of cold water. Bring to a simmer and cook for 12 minutes. Drain. When the eggs are cool enough to handle, peel and coarsely chop. Set aside.

3. Baste the naan with 1 tablespoon of olive oil and sprinkle with ¼ teaspoon each of salt and pepper. Place on a rimmed baking sheet and lightly toast in the oven for 8 to 10 minutes.

4. While the naan is toasting, heat the remaining 1 tablespoon of olive oil in a medium skillet over medium heat. Add the leeks and asparagus, and sauté until softened, 8 to 10 minutes. Stir in the thyme and season with the remaining ¾ teaspoon of salt and ¼ teaspoon of pepper. Transfer to a medium bowl and toss with 3 tablespoons of vinaigrette.

5. Spread the ricotta across the naan, and top with the dressed leeks and asparagus and the chopped eggs.

6. Serve with a final drizzle of the remaining 1 tablespoon of vinaigrette, a few sprinkles of freshly ground pepper, and the Parmesan cheese.

SUBSTITUTION TIP: Use 1½ cups thinly sliced scallions instead of the leeks.

PER SERVING: CALORIES: 620; TOTAL FAT: 38G; TOTAL CARBS: 32G; FIBER: 4G; SUGAR: 6G; PROTEIN: 19G; SODIUM: 1929MG

MIDDLE EASTERN CAULIFLOWER STEAKS

Prep time: 5 minutes • **Cook time:** 25 minutes

Cauliflower steaks are one of the easiest vegetarian entrées to make and, like beef steaks, can be dressed up with a wide variety of sauces and spices. In fact, most of the sauces in the Kitchen Staples chapter (page 167) can be served with these cauliflower steaks for an entrée ready in less than 30 minutes. The 15-minute prep time assumes you have the hummus and chermoula on hand, or that you'll make them while the cauliflower steaks roast. Although you can get away with a store-bought hummus substitute, trust me when I say you'll want to make the chermoula yourself. **SERVES 4**

Dairy-free • Gluten-free • Vegan

1 large head cauliflower

1 tablespoon olive oil

½ teaspoon kosher salt

¼ teaspoon freshly ground black pepper

¼ cup Smooth and Creamy Hummus (page 176) or store-bought

2 tablespoons Lemony Moroccan Chermoula Sauce (page 172)

½ cup coarsely crushed peanuts

1. Preheat the oven to 425°F.

2. Cut off the cauliflower stems and remove all leaves at the base. Place the head cut-side down and slice it in half down the middle. Starting from that cut, begin to slice each half into ¾-inch-thick steaks—any thinner will make it difficult for them to hold together as steaks. As you reach the rounded edge, you'll have loose florets.

3. Arrange the cauliflower steaks on a baking sheet in a single layer and place the loose florets around them. Drizzle with the olive oil and sprinkle with the salt and pepper. Bake until golden brown, 20 to 25 minutes. They'll be lightly browned, and tender when pierced with a knife. Take them out before they become completely limp.

4. If you don't have the hummus or chermoula on hand, make them now. This will increase the prep time on the recipe but not the overall time, since you can prep them while the cauliflower roasts.

5. Spread the hummus on each steak, using about 2 teaspoons for the largest steaks. Drizzle with the chermoula and top with the peanuts. The loose roasted florets can be added on top with the peanuts.

PER SERVING: CALORIES: 167; TOTAL FAT: 13G; TOTAL CARBS: 10G; FIBER: 4G; SUGAR: 2G; PROTEIN: 6G; SODIUM: 337MG

WARM SWEET POTATO NOODLE SALAD

Prep time: 20 minutes • **Cook time:** 7 minutes

When I'm feeling lazy, I buy already spiralized sweet potatoes from the produce section of my market. If you don't have that option but you have a spiralizer, you can make your own! First peel the potatoes, as the consistency of sweet potato pasta is better without the skin. Cut off both ends of the potatoes and insert the small spaghetti blade. Affix the potatoes onto the spiralizer and make your noodles. **SERVES 4**

Gluten-free: Use gluten-free tamari

4 tablespoons Miso Butter (page 174)

2 tablespoons ginger paste or finely grated fresh ginger

1 teaspoon garlic paste or minced garlic

2 tablespoons olive oil

2 cups spiralized sweet potato noodles (from about 2 large sweet potatoes)

2 (5-ounce) bags baby spinach

1½ cups Crispy Spicy Chickpeas (page 169)

1 bunch scallions, thinly sliced

1 avocado, cut into chunks

1 to 2 teaspoons tamari or low-sodium soy sauce

1. Combine the miso butter, ginger, and garlic in a small bowl. Set aside.

2. Heat the olive oil and 2 tablespoons of the miso butter mixture in a well-seasoned cast iron pan or a nonstick skillet over medium heat. Add the sweet potato noodles. Use tongs to gently toss the noodles and coat them in the butter. Cook for 5 to 7 minutes, occasionally tossing the noodles. They'll start to collapse into the skillet after about 3 minutes, but should retain their shape and height. The finished noodles should be tender with a little crunch. If the skillet dries out, add another tablespoon of the miso butter mixture.

3. While the noodles are cooking, combine the spinach, chickpeas, scallions, and avocado in a large bowl. When the sweet potato noodles are ready, add them to the bowl along with 1 tablespoon of the miso butter mixture, if needed, and the tamari. Using your hands, toss the salad to coat the spinach with the miso butter and soy sauce. Taste and season with additional miso butter or tamari, if needed. Serve warm.

FLEXITARIAN TIP: Either grill or broil flank steak that has been well-seasoned with salt and pepper. Thinly slice across the grain and place on top of the warm salad.

PER SERVING: CALORIES: 426; TOTAL FAT: 24G; TOTAL CARBS: 45G; FIBER: 13G; SUGAR: 6G; PROTEIN: 11G; SODIUM: 882MG

CHOPPED KALE SALAD WITH APPLES AND PUMPKIN SEEDS

Prep time: 10 minutes • **Cook time:** 5 minutes

Most people go to the Cheesecake Factory for their incredible selection of towering cheesecakes. I go there for their kale salad and crave it when it's been too long between visits. It features frilly kale leaves tossed with tender-crisp green beans and tiny apple cubes, with a buttermilk dressing. When we moved to an area that meant a longer drive to one of their restaurants, down a windy mountain road that often closes during the winter, I realized I had to create my own version. **SERVES 4**

Gluten-free • Nut-free

2 cups green beans, halved

8 cups thinly sliced curly kale leaves

2 cups store-bought shredded broccoli slaw

½ cup dried cranberries

½ cup Roasted Pumpkin Seeds (page 170)

2 Granny Smith apples, cored and chopped

¼ cup ranch dressing

Freshly ground black pepper

2 tablespoons grated Parmesan cheese

1. Fill a medium pot with 2 inches of water and insert a steamer basket. Put the beans in the basket, cover, and bring the water to a boil. Reduce the heat to a simmer and steam the beans until tender, about 5 minutes. Transfer the beans to a colander and immediately douse them with cold water until cool.

2. In a large bowl, combine the kale with the broccoli slaw, cranberries, pumpkin seeds, apples, and cooked beans. Drizzle with the dressing and toss to coat, adding more to taste.

3. Season the salad with black pepper and serve topped with the Parmesan cheese.

SUBSTITUTION TIP: For a lighter dressing, use the Lemon Vinaigrette (page 15), or do an Asian twist with the Tahini Miso Dressing (page 179).

PER SERVING: CALORIES: 291; TOTAL FAT: 10G; TOTAL CARBS: 46G; FIBER: 8G; SUGAR: 18G; PROTEIN: 9G; SODIUM: 236MG

FRESH AND HEARTY QUINOA SALAD

Prep time: 10 minutes • **Cook time:** 5 minutes

I like to add a little nutritional yeast to soups, salads, and casseroles for an additional punch of protein and nutrition. An inactive yeast (meaning you can't use it as a leavener when baking), nutritional yeast is considered a complete protein and offers benefits for digestion and immunity functions. Used in small amounts, it doesn't much affect the flavor of a dish, but in larger quantities, it's a great stand-in for cheese with its nutty, savory flavor. **SERVES 2**

Dairy-free • **Gluten-free** • **Nut-free** • **Vegan**

1 tablespoon olive oil

¾ cup thinly sliced scallions

½ cup cooked quinoa
(see page 55)

1 (15-ounce) can black beans,
drained and rinsed

1 teaspoon garlic paste or
minced garlic

1 teaspoon ground cumin

½ cup halved red grapes

1 tablespoon freshly squeezed
lime juice or rice vinegar

1 avocado, diced

¼ teaspoon kosher salt

¼ teaspoon freshly ground
black pepper

1 tablespoon nutritional yeast

1. Heat the olive oil in a medium skillet over medium heat. Add the scallions, quinoa, beans, garlic, cumin, and grapes. Cook until fragrant, about 5 minutes. Remove the skillet from the heat.

2. Place the quinoa mixture in a serving bowl and toss with the lime juice, avocado, salt, pepper, and nutritional yeast.

PER SERVING: CALORIES: 647; TOTAL FAT: 30G; TOTAL CARBS: 78G; FIBER: 27G; SUGAR: 8G; PROTEIN: 25G; SODIUM: 311MG

How to Make Perfect Quinoa

The two most common types of quinoa are red and white. White quinoa has a milder, earthier flavor and cooks up a little more quickly than the red. Both types have an outer coating, called saponin, which can impart a bitter, soapy flavor. Most boxed quinoa is prerinsed, but I still rinse it before adding it to the pot unless I plan to use it in a soup or casserole. To rinse, place 1 cup of quinoa in a fine-mesh strainer or colander and run cold water over it for 1 to 2 minutes while lightly rubbing the quinoa seeds between your hands to remove the saponin.

Cooking quinoa is easy. Here's how to do it.

2 cups water or vegetable broth
½ teaspoon kosher salt
1 cup quinoa

1. Set a pot on the stove over medium-high heat. Add the water or broth and salt to the pot and bring to a boil.

2. Add the quinoa and reduce the heat to a simmer.

3. Cover the pot and cook until the liquid is completely absorbed, about 15 minutes. The quinoa is done when you see curlicues pop up in the cooked seed.

IF YOU WANT YOUR QUINOA FLUFFIER: For example, for a salad that will be dressed—cook the quinoa uncovered. Once the liquid is absorbed, remove the pot from the heat and cover it for 5 minutes to allow it to steam.

SUMMER TOMATO AND BURRATA PANZANELLA SALAD

Prep time: 15 minutes • **Cook time:** 15 minutes

Panzanella is a peasant bread salad, which likely originated in Italy as a way to use stale bread. The version that I'm most familiar with is nothing more than ripe, juicy tomatoes chopped and sprinkled with some salt and pepper. They're joined in a bowl with some crusty hard bread and a few slices of sweet onion for at least 30 minutes to stew in the natural juices, and finished with a drizzle of olive oil and a splash of vinegar. Letting the salad sit for 2 hours or even longer only makes it better. So if you have a little extra time, just let this sit on the counter while you relax. I've added some chickpeas and burrata mozzarella to the recipe to give it a little extra punch of protein. **SERVES 2**

Nut-free

2 tablespoons balsamic vinegar

1¼ teaspoons kosher salt, divided

½ teaspoon freshly ground black pepper, plus ⅛ teaspoon

6 tablespoons olive oil, divided

4 cups chopped tomatoes

1 (15-ounce) can chickpeas, drained and rinsed

½ sweet onion, thinly sliced

2 tablespoons thinly sliced fresh basil

3 (1-inch-thick) slices crusty bread, such as ciabatta

1 teaspoon garlic paste or minced garlic

2 balls burrata mozzarella cheese, torn into 4 to 6 pieces

1. Preheat the oven to 400°F. Line a rimmed baking sheet with parchment paper.

2. In a large bowl, whisk together the vinegar, 1 teaspoon of salt, ½ teaspoon of black pepper, and 3 tablespoons of olive oil. Add the tomatoes, chickpeas, onion, and basil, and toss to evenly coat. Set aside.

3. Tear or cut the bread into large pieces, about 2 inches across. Add the remaining 3 tablespoons of olive oil to a large bowl and stir in the garlic. Toss the bread with the garlic and olive oil and arrange in a single layer on the baking sheet. Season the bread with the remaining ¼ teaspoon of salt and remaining ⅛ teaspoon of pepper. Bake for 10 minutes. Turn the bread pieces over and bake for another 5 minutes.

4. To serve, place the pieces of burrata on a serving plate. Toss the toasted bread with the tomato salad and pour everything over the burrata, including any residual dressing.

PER SERVING: CALORIES: 935; TOTAL FAT: 55G; TOTAL CARBS: 88G; FIBER: 18G; SUGAR: 17G; PROTEIN: 29G; SODIUM: 1961MG

LEBANESE LENTIL SALAD

Prep time: 15 minutes • **Cook time:** 15 minutes

When I lived in Boston, one of my closest friends there was half Lebanese. Thanks to her and her wonderful family, who invited me over for just about every holiday, I learned a lot about the food of Lebanon. Although lamb is a favorite food there, Lebanese food is also known for its wide variety of vegetables, often simply dressed with olive oil, lemon, salt, and pepper. In this recipe, earthy lentils marry well with sherry vinegar, but feel free to substitute lemon if you can't find it, or make the Lemony Moroccan Chermoula Sauce (page 172). **SERVES 4**

Gluten-free • **Nut-free**

3 cups vegetable broth or water

1 cup French green lentils

1 teaspoon kosher salt, divided

3 tablespoons sherry vinegar

1 teaspoon Dijon mustard

2 tablespoons olive oil

3 scallions, thinly sliced

2 cups peeled and diced cucumber

1½ cups halved cherry tomatoes

½ cup crumbled feta cheese

¼ cup fresh mint leaves, thinly sliced

¼ teaspoon freshly ground black pepper

1. Bring the broth to a boil in a medium pot. Add the lentils and ½ teaspoon of salt. Reduce the heat to a simmer, cover, and simmer for 15 to 20 minutes, or until the lentils are tender and the liquid is absorbed. If there is any liquid remaining, drain it.

2. In a large bowl, whisk together the sherry vinegar and Dijon mustard. Whisk in the olive oil until emulsified. Add the cooked lentils, scallions, cucumber, tomatoes, feta cheese, and mint, and toss to coat. Season to taste with the remaining ½ teaspoon of salt and the pepper. Serve at room temperature.

FLEXITARIAN TIP: This salad is great with lamb chops. Season the chops on both sides with salt and pepper, and sauté in a little olive oil over medium-high heat. Cook for about 3 minutes on each side for medium-rare, depending on the thickness of the chops.

PER SERVING: CALORIES: 337; TOTAL FAT: 13G; TOTAL CARBS: 36G; FIBER: 17G; SUGAR: 5G; PROTEIN: 20G; SODIUM: 1389MG

CHICKPEA NIÇOISE SALAD

Prep time: 10 minutes • **Cook time:** 17 minutes

Niçoise salad is what I think of as France's version of our American Cobb salad. It's one of my go-to party dishes for guests to enjoy while we sit around a table outside sipping wine. Most of this salad is assembled while the potatoes and beans are cooking, so it's all ready to serve in less than 30 minutes. **SERVES 4**

Dairy-free • Gluten-free • Nut-free

½ cup Lemony Moroccan Chermoula Sauce (page 172)

3 large eggs

1 tablespoon kosher salt

1 pound small red or fingerling potatoes

½ pound green beans, trimmed

1 head Bibb lettuce

2 (15-ounce) cans chickpeas, drained and rinsed

1 (6-ounce) jar marinated artichokes, drained

½ cup halved cherry tomatoes

½ cup Niçoise or Kalamata olives

1. Put the chermoula sauce in a large bowl and set aside.

2. Put the eggs in a small pot and cover them with at least 1 inch of water. Bring to a low boil over medium-high heat. Reduce the heat to medium to maintain a simmer. Simmer the eggs for 12 minutes, then remove them from the pot. When the eggs are cool enough to handle, peel them.

3. While the eggs are cooking, fill a medium pot with 2 inches of water and the salt. Insert a steamer basket in the pot, and put the potatoes in the basket. Bring to a boil over medium-high heat. Cover with a lid and reduce the heat to medium-low to maintain a steady low boil. Cook until the potatoes are tender, 10 to 12 minutes, depending on the size of the potatoes.

4. Using tongs, transfer the potatoes to the bowl of chermoula, leaving the steamer basket and water in the pot. Toss the warm potatoes to coat in the sauce.

5. Add the beans to the steamer basket. Cover and simmer until tender, about 5 minutes. Transfer the beans to the bowl with the potatoes and sauce, and toss to coat.

6. Spread the lettuce leaves on a serving plate. Arrange the chickpeas, artichokes, cherry tomatoes, and olives on the lettuce, leaving enough room for the eggs, potatoes, and beans.

7. Slice the eggs in half lengthwise and place on the lettuce. Remove the potatoes and beans from the chermoula, arrange on the lettuce, and drizzle the remaining chermoula over the entire salad. Serve at room temperature.

INGREDIENT TIP: If you have extra time, add crispy baked tofu to the recipe. Just follow the instructions on page 134.

FLEXITARIAN TIP: For my nonvegetarian guests, I add canned albacore tuna drizzled with olive oil and lemon juice, and serve it all with small toasted slices of French bread for crostini. Sliced cheeses, crackers, and fancy spreads complete the table.

SUBSTITUTION TIP: In place of the chermoula, you can substitute a store-bought aioli or vinaigrette, or make the Easy Roasted Red Pepper Aioli (page 177).

PER SERVING: CALORIES: 572; TOTAL FAT: 31G; TOTAL CARBS: 63G; FIBER: 18G; SUGAR: 9G; PROTEIN: 21G; SODIUM: 2160MG

GRILLED MEDITERRANEAN SALAD WITH QUINOA

Prep time: 15 minutes • **Cook time:** 12 minutes

Many people complain that eggplant is bitter. There are a few ways to manage and avoid this. A common solution is to salt slices of eggplant and allow them to drain for 30 minutes. Another option is to peel the eggplant. If you're rushed for time, skip the salting and instead purchase smaller eggplant, such as Chinese or Asian varieties. Seeds affect bitterness, and these varieties have less of them. Additionally, the longer and thinner the eggplant, the less bitter it will be. **SERVES 4**

Dairy-free • Gluten-free • Nut-free • Vegan

1 small eggplant, peeled and sliced into ½-inch rounds

3 tablespoons olive oil, divided

1 medium zucchini, sliced into long strips

2 yellow summer squash, sliced into long strips

2 bell peppers, any color, sliced into thick strips

4 scallions

1½ teaspoons kosher salt, divided

1 teaspoon freshly ground black pepper, divided

2 cups cooked quinoa (see page 55)

¼ cup Lemon Vinaigrette (page 15)

¼ cup thinly sliced basil

1. Preheat the grill.

2. Baste both sides of the eggplant slices with a little olive oil, and toss the strips of zucchini, summer squash, bell peppers, and scallions with the remaining oil. Season with the salt and pepper.

3. Arrange the vegetables on a vegetable grill pan designed for a gas grill, with the eggplant and bell peppers on one side of the pan and the zucchini, summer squash, and scallions on the other. Adjust the flame to medium heat. Grill for 4 minutes, then turn over the faster-cooking squash and scallions. Grill for another 2 minutes, then flip over the eggplant and bell peppers. Continue to grill the vegetables until they're tender and slightly charred. This might take another 2 or 3 minutes for the zucchini, squash, and scallions and 4 to 6 minutes for the eggplant and peppers. Transfer to a cutting board.

4. Slice the eggplant, zucchini, summer squash, bell peppers, and scallions into bite-size chunks and place in a large bowl. Add the quinoa, drizzle with the vinaigrette, and toss to coat.

5. Serve topped with the basil.

INGREDIENT TIP: If you make a dip or sauce with eggplant, soak the eggplant slices in milk for 30 minutes before preparing the recipe. This not only tempers the bitterness, it also makes the end result beautifully creamy.

FLEXITARIAN TIP: Season flank steak with salt and pepper, and grill alongside the vegetables. Thinly slice across the grain and serve with the salad.

COOKING TIP: If you don't have a grill, this salad can be made on the stove top using a grill pan, griddle, or large skillet. Depending on the size of your pan, you may need to sauté each ingredient separately in batches. The other option is to roast the veggies using two sheet pans. One sheet pan holds the zucchini, squash, and scallions, and the other one holds the eggplant and peppers. Roast at 400°F until tender, about 15 minutes for the zucchini, squash, and scallions and 30 minutes for the eggplant and peppers.

PER SERVING: CALORIES: 395; TOTAL FAT: 19G; TOTAL CARBS: 50G; FIBER: 10G; SUGAR: 12G; PROTEIN: 10G; SODIUM: 1145MG

TORTILLA SOUP

Prep time: 10 minutes • **Cook time:** 15 minutes

Some of my kitchen experiments make me want to hide in the closet. Others make me feel like I should have my own show on the Food Network. This one, thankfully, falls closer to the Food Network than the closet. I often purchase salsa for a party but then have a lot left over. Eventually it goes bad, and I throw it out. Then I throw another party and start all over. This soup was created when I was out of tomatoes but had a lot of salsa in the refrigerator. I recommend using a salsa with at least medium heat, as the spice becomes diluted in the soup. **SERVES 4**

Gluten-free • Nut-free

1 tablespoon olive oil

1 tablespoon garlic paste or minced garlic

1 teaspoon chili powder

2 (15-ounce) cans black beans, drained and rinsed

2 cups vegetable broth or Better Than Bouillon No Chicken Base

1 cup fresh or frozen corn kernels

1 (15-ounce) jar salsa

Kosher salt (optional)

Freshly ground black pepper (optional)

½ cup shredded mix of Mexican cheeses, for garnish

½ cup thinly sliced scallions, for garnish

½ avocado, diced, for garnish

1 cup crumbled tortilla chips, for garnish

Lime wedges, for serving

1. In a large, heavy-bottomed pot, warm the olive oil over medium heat. Add the garlic and chili powder and cook until very fragrant, about 1 minute.

2. Stir in the black beans, broth, corn, and salsa. Bring to a simmer and cook for 10 minutes. Season to taste with salt and pepper (if using).

3. Serve garnished with the cheese, scallions, avocado, and tortilla chips, with lime wedges on the side.

FLEXITARIAN TIP: Purchase a pre-roasted chicken and dice the breast meat. Stir into the soup in step 2.

PER SERVING: CALORIES: 369; TOTAL FAT: 14G; TOTAL CARBS: 48G; FIBER: 15G; SUGAR: 5G; PROTEIN: 20G; SODIUM: 1135MG

CHEESY BROCCOLI SOUP

Prep time: 15 minutes • **Cook time:** 15 minutes

Some apples are excellent for pies, cobblers, or other baked dishes in which you want them to hold their shape through the baking process. Others fall apart into applesauce, and cook even further down to apple butter. The best apples for this recipe are ones you would use to make applesauce, such as Gravenstein, McIntosh, or Golden Delicious. Honeycrisp and Gala apples work well, too. **SERVES 4**

Gluten-free • Nut-free
Dairy-free and Vegan: Skip the cheese and add up to ½ cup nutritional yeast

2 tablespoons olive oil

1 yellow onion, diced

1 pound broccoli, cut into 1-inch florets and stems thinly sliced

2 large apples, peeled, cored, and coarsely chopped

1 teaspoon kosher salt

½ teaspoon freshly ground black pepper

3 cups vegetable broth

½ cup shredded Cheddar cheese, plus more for serving

Apple cider vinegar or freshly squeezed lemon juice (optional, to taste)

1. Heat the olive oil in a large, heavy-bottomed pot over medium-high heat. Add the onion and sauté until softened, about 5 minutes. Add the broccoli, apples, salt, pepper, and broth. Bring to a rapid boil, cover, reduce the heat to low, and simmer for 10 to 15 minutes, or until the broccoli is tender.

2. Use an immersion blender to purée the soup. Alternatively, transfer the soup to a blender (in batches, if necessary) and purée, then return the soup to the pot.

3. Stir in the cheese and season to taste with additional salt and pepper, if needed. Add a little apple cider vinegar to sharpen the flavors (if desired).

4. Serve hot with additional cheese for the cheese lovers in your family, and crusty bread if gluten isn't something you're avoiding.

PER SERVING: CALORIES: 238; TOTAL FAT: 13G; TOTAL CARBS: 28G; FIBER: 7G; SUGAR: 16G; PROTEIN: 7G; SODIUM: 1107MG

BUTTERNUT SQUASH SOUP WITH APPLE CIDER

Prep time: 10 minutes • **Cook time:** 20 minutes

I've never yet met a butternut squash soup I didn't love, but I begin every autumn with this version. I come back to it time after time because it comes together so quickly. The finishing touch of a dollop of crème fraîche is optional, but I find that it balances the sweetness of the squash and apple cider. It can be found in the dairy case near either sour cream or mascarpone in most markets. For bonus flavor or savory crunch, I sometimes add chopped parsley, almonds, sunflower kernels, or even a handful of Crispy Spicy Chickpeas (page 169) as a garnish. **SERVES 6**

Gluten-free
Dairy-free and Vegan: Omit the crème fraîche
Nut-free: Omit the almonds for topping

2 tablespoons olive oil

2 cups diced yellow onion

10 cups (1-inch) cubed
butternut squash

4 cups vegetable broth

1 cup apple cider

1 teaspoon kosher salt

OPTIONAL TOPPINGS

¼ cup crème fraîche

2 tablespoons sliced almonds

1 tablespoon salted
sunflower seeds

1 tablespoon chopped
fresh parsley

2 tablespoons Crispy Spicy
Chickpeas (page 169)

1. In a large, heavy-bottomed pot, heat the oil over medium-high heat. Add the onion and sauté until it begins to soften, about 5 minutes.

2. Add the squash, broth, cider, and salt. Bring to a simmer and cook until the squash becomes tender, about 15 minutes.

3. Use an immersion blender to purée into a smooth, silky soup. Alternatively, pour the soup into a blender (in batches, if necessary) and purée.

4. Serve in bowls with a dollop of crème fraîche, if using. Garnish with a sprinkling of one or more of the optional toppings, if desired.

PER SERVING: CALORIES: 151; TOTAL FAT: 5G; TOTAL CARBS: 27G; FIBER: 5G; SUGAR: 11G; PROTEIN: 2G; SODIUM: 744MG

BLACK BEAN AND QUINOA WRAP

Prep time: 10 minutes • **Cook time:** 15 minutes

Years ago, I took daylong hikes in the hills every weekend as a way to rebalance myself after a hard week of work in the city. It kept me sane, giving me the time and space I needed to be alone and think. I didn't want to cut my time in nature short because I was hungry, so I started making tortilla wraps, rolled up in aluminum foil, that were easy to throw into my backpack along with an apple and a zipped bag of roasted pumpkin seeds. If you have a stash of cooked quinoa and hummus in the refrigerator, this wrap can come together in less than 10 minutes. **SERVES 4**

Dairy-free • **Nut-free**
Gluten-free and Vegan: Use corn tortillas or romaine lettuce leaves as wraps

⅔ cup cooked quinoa (see page 55)

1 (15-ounce) can black beans, drained and rinsed

1 teaspoon garlic powder

⅔ cup quartered cherry tomatoes

2 tablespoons freshly squeezed lime juice

½ teaspoon kosher salt

¼ cup Smooth and Creamy Hummus (page 176) or store-bought

4 (8-inch) flour tortillas

½ cup baby spinach leaves

1. In a medium pot, combine the cooked quinoa with the beans and garlic powder and warm through over medium-low heat. Remove the pot from the heat and stir in the tomatoes, lime juice, and salt.

2. Spread the hummus evenly on each tortilla, lightly cover with spinach leaves, and spoon about ⅓ cup of the quinoa mixture in a heaped row, slightly off center, across the tortilla. Fold one side of the tortilla over the quinoa and roll up fairly tightly. Use a toothpick to hold it closed or wrap in aluminum foil.

PER SERVING: CALORIES: 342; TOTAL FAT: 6G; TOTAL CARBS: 58G; FIBER: 11G; SUGAR: 2G; PROTEIN: 15G; SODIUM: 756MG

SPICY CHICKPEA GYROS

Prep time: 15 minutes

This recipe is a perfect example of a meal coming together in minutes when you have a pantry of useful ingredients and condiments on hand. But even if you don't, the chickpeas can be roasted for this recipe in 20 minutes. You can whip up the tzatziki, and let it sit while they roast. You've still got a great meal in less than 30 minutes. **SERVES 4**

Nut-free

2 slices naan bread, halved, or whole pita rounds

1 cup Tzatziki (page 175)

1½ cups Crispy Spicy Chickpeas (page 169)

4 Bibb lettuce leaves

1 large tomato, chopped

¼ red onion, thinly sliced

1. Lay the halved naan slices on a flat workspace and divide the tzatziki among them, spreading it across the surface. Layer the chickpeas, lettuce, tomato, and red onion on top of each naan half.

2. Fold the naan in half around the filling, and serve with extra tzatziki.

FLEXITARIAN TIP: Sauté a few lamb loin chops in a medium skillet and slice off the meat to add to the gyro with, or instead of, the chickpeas. Depending on the thickness of the chops, cooking for 3 minutes on each side over medium-high heat will result in medium-rare meat. Other cuts of lamb are equally suitable but take longer to cook.

PER SERVING: CALORIES: 120; TOTAL FAT: 5G; TOTAL CARBS: 16G; FIBER: 3G; SUGAR: 2G; PROTEIN: 5G; SODIUM: 120MG

BLACK BEAN TOSTADA WITH DELICATA SQUASH

Prep time: 15 minutes • **Cook time:** 15 minutes

Delicata squash is the fat, cigar-shaped squash that looks like a yellow zeppelin with green stripes. I walked by them for years without a clue what to do with them. After trying them at some trendy restaurant in San Francisco, I finally took the plunge. To my delight, I found them super easy to work with. Genetically, they're in the same family as summer squash like zucchini, yellow crookneck, and pattypan, and, like them, their thin skin facilitates easy slicing, eliminating the need to peel. They have a milder flavor than winter squash, and can be stuffed, roasted, or sautéed with great ease. **SERVES 6**

Dairy-free • **Gluten-free** • **Nut-free**

1 small Delicata squash, seeded and pulp removed, cut into ½-inch cubes

1 tablespoon olive oil

½ teaspoon kosher salt

¼ teaspoon freshly ground black pepper

2 cups cauliflower rice

2 (15-ounce) cans black beans, drained and rinsed

½ small head purple cabbage, shredded or thinly sliced

½ jalapeño pepper, seeded and minced

3 tablespoons Lime Vinaigrette (page 178)

6 tostada shells (see Ingredient tip)

1. Preheat the oven to 400°F. Line a rimmed baking sheet with parchment paper.

2. Arrange the squash in a single layer on the baking sheet. Drizzle with the olive oil and sprinkle with the salt and pepper. Roast for 15 minutes, or until tender.

3. In a large bowl, place the cauliflower rice, beans, cabbage, and jalapeño, and toss with the vinaigrette.

4. Place a tostada shell on each plate, and divide the cauliflower rice mixture among the shells. Top with the roasted squash.

INGREDIENT TIP: If you can't find tostada shells in your market, make your own with corn tortillas. Place 6 tortillas on a baking sheet. Brush both sides with olive oil and sprinkle with salt. Bake in the oven with the Delicata squash for 8 minutes, turning the tortillas over after 4 minutes. Remove and let cool. They'll continue to crisp up while they cool.

SUBSTITUTION TIP: If you can't find Delicata squash in your market, substitute with ½-inch cubes of peeled butternut squash.

PER SERVING: CALORIES: 347; TOTAL FAT: 13G; TOTAL CARBS: 51G; FIBER: 11G; SUGAR: 3G; PROTEIN: 10G; SODIUM: 502MG

GENIUS ASPARAGUS PASTA

Prep time: 2 minutes • **Cook time:** 13 minutes

Quick cooking is what elevates this pasta to genius status. Technically known as an *absorption* pasta, you'd typically cook it the same way as risotto, by adding a cup of hot broth and letting the pasta absorb it before ladling in another cup. But I like to add enough broth from the start, put a lid on it, and do something else while it simmers. The pasta is done before the traditional large pasta pot has even come to a boil, saving you time, water, and cooking gas. At the end you have a sexy, silky pasta coated with broth and natural pasta starches, needing little more than a flurry of Parmesan and freshly ground pepper. **SERVES 2**

Nut-free
Dairy-free and Vegan: Use nutritional yeast in place of the cheese

1 tablespoon olive oil

1 tablespoon garlic paste or minced garlic

4 ounces (a little less than 2 cups) short, sturdy pasta, such as farfalle

1½ cups vegetable broth or Better Than Bouillon Seasoned Vegetable Base

¼ teaspoon kosher salt

½ pound asparagus, trimmed and cut into 1-inch lengths

Freshly ground black pepper

1 tablespoon grated Parmesan cheese

1. Heat the olive oil in a large skillet over medium heat. Add the garlic and cook for 1 minute. Add the pasta and cook, stirring occasionally, for another 2 minutes.

2. Pour in the broth and add the salt. The pasta must be covered by the broth, so add a little more if necessary. Bring to a boil, then reduce the heat to medium-low or low. (I heat my broth first in the microwave to get it hot faster and save a little time.) Cover and maintain a simmer for 10 minutes, or until the pasta is al dente. After the first 5 minutes, add the asparagus.

3. Ladle the pasta and asparagus into a bowl, with a little of the broth. Top with freshly ground black pepper and the Parmesan cheese.

SUBSTITUTION TIP: Substitute any fast-cooking vegetable for the asparagus, such as chopped zucchini or yellow squash.

PER SERVING: CALORIES: 348; TOTAL FAT: 8G; TOTAL CARBS: 46G; FIBER: 7G; SUGAR: 6G; PROTEIN: 16G; SODIUM: 836MG

COUSCOUS PRIMAVERA WITH CHICKPEAS

Prep time: 15 minutes • **Cook time:** 10 minutes

I have three main approaches to vegetable broth: (1) I make my own and freeze it in zipped plastic bags, (2) I buy it already made, and (3) I use one of several Better Than Bouillon products. When I need the broth to contribute some deep flavor, I go with option 3 and eliminate any other salt from the recipe. In this recipe, Better Than Bouillon amps up the flavor of the couscous and the entire dish. I buy it from my local market, but you can purchase it online and have it delivered right to your door. It's packed with rich flavor, keeps for a long time in the refrigerator, and is easy to measure out and use. **4 SERVINGS**

Dairy-free • Nut-free • Vegan

2 cups couscous

2 cups asparagus, trimmed and cut into ½-inch pieces

1 cup fresh or thawed frozen peas

½ cup chopped scallions

¼ teaspoon freshly ground black pepper

½ teaspoon kosher salt (optional)

2 cups vegetable broth or 1 teaspoon Better Than Bouillon Seasoned Vegetable Base

¼ cup chopped fresh mint

1 cup Crispy Spicy Chickpeas (page 169)

1. Place the couscous in a 12-by-12-inch baking dish. Layer the asparagus, peas, and scallions over the couscous, and sprinkle everything with the pepper. If you will be using broth, sprinkle the salt over everything, too, but skip the salt if you use Better Than Bouillon.

2. Bring the broth to a boil in a small pot. If using Better Than Bouillon, dilute it in 8 ounces of boiling water. Pour the broth over the couscous and vegetable mixture. Immediately cover the baking dish tightly with plastic wrap and let sit for 10 minutes.

3. Add the mint and fluff the couscous with a fork. Top with the chickpeas. Serve warm.

FLEXITARIAN TIP: Sauté shrimp seasoned with salt, pepper, and smoked paprika on the stove top, and add at the end with, or in place of, the chickpeas.

PER SERVING: CALORIES: 463; TOTAL FAT: 3G; TOTAL CARBS: 89G; FIBER: 12G; SUGAR: 6G; PROTEIN: 21G; SODIUM: 718MG

SPRINGTIME FREGOLA WITH BROCCOLI, PEAS, AND EGGS

Prep time: 5 minutes • **Cook time:** 25 minutes

Fregola, also spelled fregula, is a Sardinian pasta made by rubbing semolina flour and water together in a circular motion to create a round shape. The pieces of pasta are then toasted in the oven. Fregola cooks up very fast like couscous, but is heavier, so I don't use them as substitutes for each other. Instead, when I can't find fregola, I use orzo, a short Italian pasta in the shape of large rice. It cooks up similarly and gives the same weight to a dish. **SERVES 4**

Nut-free

1¼ cups fregola or orzo

3 large eggs

2 cups finely chopped broccoli florets

1 cup frozen peas

1 tablespoon olive oil

2 tablespoons capers

1 teaspoon garlic paste or minced garlic

1 tablespoon freshly squeezed lemon juice

¼ teaspoon kosher salt

4 ounces part-skim ricotta cheese

Freshly ground black pepper

Lemony Breadcrumbs (page 171; optional)

1. Bring a pot of well-salted water to a boil. Add the fregola and cook according to the package directions, until al dente. Drain.

2. Meanwhile, place the eggs in a medium pot and cover with cold water by about 2 inches. Bring to a simmer, cover, and cook for 10 minutes. Use tongs to remove the eggs (but keep the water simmering) and place the eggs in a bowl of ice water to halt any further cooking. Once cool enough to handle, peel the eggs and finely chop or grate on the large holes of a box grater.

3. Partially empty the pot of simmering water, leaving just enough to steam the broccoli and peas. Place a steamer insert in the bottom of the pot, and put the broccoli and peas in the insert. Cover and steam until tender, about 10 minutes. Set aside.

4. Empty the pot completely of water and return it to the stove over medium heat. Heat the olive oil, then add the capers and garlic. Sauté until fragrant, about 1 minute. Add the broccoli and peas, lemon juice, and salt. Sauté and toss together for 2 minutes.

5. To serve, spread the fregola on a plate and top with the broccoli mixture, followed by the grated eggs, a dollop of ricotta, and a twist of freshly ground pepper. Finish with a flurry of breadcrumbs (if using).

COOKING TIP: If you have hard-boiled eggs on hand, you can use them and skip the cooking in step 2.

FLEXITARIAN TIP: Toss strips of prosciutto into the fregola with the broccoli and peas in step 4.

PER SERVING: CALORIES: 238; TOTAL FAT: 10G; TOTAL CARBS: 24G; FIBER: 4G; SUGAR: 4G; PROTEIN: 14G; SODIUM: 407MG

SMASHED CHICKPEA AND KALAMATA PASTA

Prep time: 5 minutes • **Cook time:** 20 minutes

Sometimes I see a recipe somewhere, in a magazine or the newspaper, and it speaks so loudly to me that I'm immediately pulled into the kitchen. This recipe is an example of that, and over the past year of making it, as often happens, I've made changes, and then changes to those changes. My inspiration for this one came from a recipe by the talented, prolific Melissa Clark in the *New York Times*, and it is one of the most flexible pasta dishes I make. I often vary it according to what I have on hand—and I invite you to do the same. **SERVES 4**

Dairy-free • Nut-free • Vegan

3 tablespoons olive oil, divided

1 teaspoon garlic paste or minced garlic

8 ounces regular or whole-wheat farfalle or other short, sturdy pasta

3 cups vegetable broth

1 teaspoon kosher salt, divided

1 (15-ounce) can chickpeas, drained and rinsed

½ yellow onion, finely diced

¼ cup thinly sliced Kalamata olives

2 tablespoons drained capers

2 jarred roasted red peppers, cut into ¼-inch-thick slices

2 tablespoons roasted red pepper packing liquid

Freshly ground black pepper

1. In a large skillet, heat 1 tablespoon of olive oil over medium heat. Add the garlic and cook until fragrant, about 1 minute. Add the pasta and cook for another 2 minutes. Add the broth and ½ teaspoon of salt. Bring to a boil, cover, and reduce the heat medium-low to maintain an active simmer. Cook for 10 minutes, or until the pasta is barely al dente. Remove the skillet from the heat, but do not drain the pasta.

2. While the pasta is cooking, place the chickpeas in a large bowl. Use a potato masher or a fork to lightly mash them; they should be about half-crushed.

3. In a medium skillet, heat the remaining 2 tablespoons of olive oil over medium heat. Add the onion and sauté until just softened, about 5 minutes. Add the olives, capers, red peppers, and remaining ½ teaspoon of salt. Continue to cook until very fragrant, 4 to 5 minutes.

4. Stir in the mashed chickpeas and the liquid from the jar of roasted red peppers. Bring to a simmer and gently cook until most of the liquid has evaporated, about 5 minutes.

5. Use a slotted spoon to transfer the cooked pasta to the skillet and add 2 to 4 tablespoons of the pasta broth liquid to create a sauce. Toss to coat the pasta, and cook for 1 to 2 minutes, adding more pasta broth if it seems too dry.

6. Serve warm seasoned with the black pepper and additional salt, if needed.

PER SERVING: CALORIES: 461; TOTAL FAT: 15G; TOTAL CARBS: 71G; FIBER: 15G; SUGAR: 9G; PROTEIN: 17G; SODIUM: 1197MG

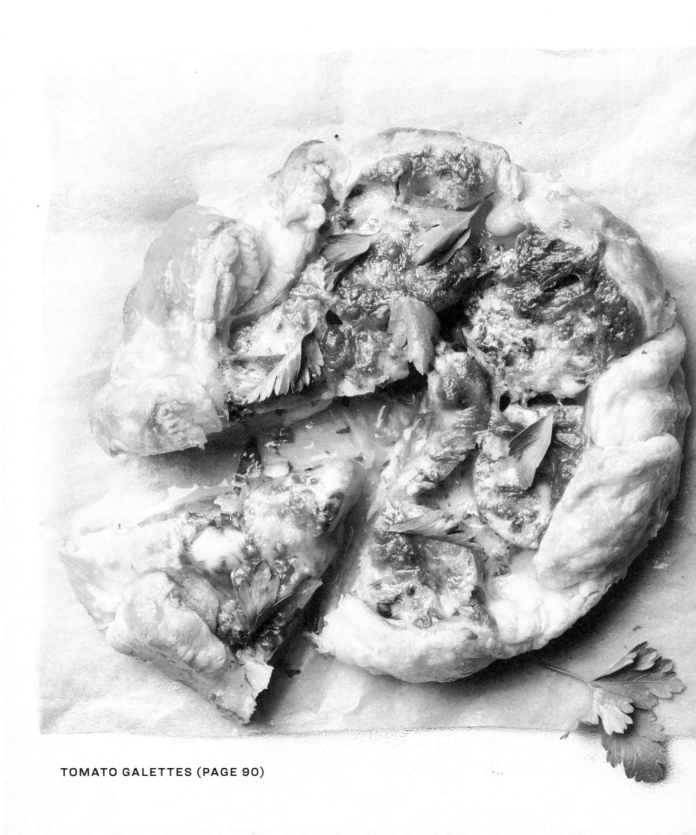

TOMATO GALETTES (PAGE 90)

4

FIVE INGREDIENTS

FLAKY HONEY BISCUITS

Prep time: 15 minutes • **Cook time:** 10 minutes

If you do a fair amount of baking, I recommend investing in a scale to weigh your flour. If you don't do that, be sure to fluff the flour with a fork before measuring. Flour compacts very easily, and without fluffing it, baked goods can be heavy, dry, and inconsistent. Serve these biscuits with the Portabella Eggs Florentine (page 44), Cheesy Broccoli Soup (page 63), Caramelized Mushrooms over Polenta (page 81), Cheddar and Broccoli-Stuffed Sweet Potatoes (page 80), or Veggie Hash with Poached Eggs (page 105). **MAKES 25 BISCUITS**

Nut-free

3 cups self-rising flour

1 teaspoon kosher salt

7 tablespoons chilled unsalted butter, cut into 1-tablespoon pats

¼ cup honey

1 cup buttermilk

1. Preheat the oven to 425°F. Line a baking sheet with parchment paper.

2. Place the flour, salt, and butter pats in the bowl of a food processor. Pulse until the butter pieces are the size of peas. Alternatively, use a pastry blender to blend the butter into the flour. Transfer the mixture to a large bowl.

3. Use your hand or a large spoon to form a well in the middle of the flour, and pour the honey and buttermilk into the well all at once. Use a spoon to fold the flour into the buttermilk and gently stir just until the mixture comes together to form a dough.

4. Lightly flour your clean countertop or a comparable flat workspace. Spill the dough and any loose flour bits onto the floured surface. Roll the dough to about a 1-inch thickness. Fold the dough in thirds, like a business envelope, and roll out again to a 1-inch thickness.

5. Stamp out biscuits using a biscuit cutter or round glass, and arrange on the baking sheet about 1 inch apart. The number of biscuits will depend on the size of your biscuit cutter/glass. I used a 1¾-inch biscuit cutter and got 25 small biscuits. A 2½-inch biscuit cutter yields 18 biscuits.

6. Bake for 8 to 10 minutes, or until lightly browned. Serve warm.

PER SERVING (1 BISCUIT): CALORIES: 97; TOTAL FAT: 3G; TOTAL CARBS: 15G; FIBER: 0G; SUGAR: 4G; PROTEIN: 2G; SODIUM: 105MG

CURRIED APPLE CHIPS

Prep time: 15 minutes • **Cook time:** 90 minutes

You can buy your own apple chips, but there's nothing better than tasting these fresh from the oven. There's little fuss involved—especially if you have a mandoline to slice the apples—with most of the time taken up by the long, slow bake. I use the second-thickest setting on my mandoline and have the apples sliced in less than a minute. Just be sure to use the safety guard or a towel when you get toward the end of the apples. Otherwise, use a sharp chef's knife. **MAKES 20 TO 25 CHIPS**

Dairy-free • Gluten-free • Nut-free • Vegan

1 tablespoon freshly squeezed lemon juice

½ cup water

2 apples, such as Fuji or Honeycrisp, cored and thinly sliced into rings

1 teaspoon curry powder

1. Preheat the oven to 200°F. Line a rimmed baking sheet with parchment paper.

2. Mix the lemon juice and water together in a medium bowl. As soon as the apples are sliced, add them to the bowl to soak for 2 minutes. Drain and pat dry with paper towels. Arrange in a single layer on the baking sheet.

3. Place the curry powder in a sieve or other sifter and lightly dust the apple slices. A little curry goes a long way, so it's not necessary to dust both sides of the apple rings.

4. Bake for 45 minutes without opening the oven. After 45 minutes, turn the slices over and bake for another 45 minutes, again without opening the oven. Since you're baking them at a low temperature, it's easy to lose the heat if you open the oven door. If you find the apple chips need additional crisping, bake for another 15 minutes.

5. For the crispiest texture, let the chips cool before eating, but they're pretty fabulous slightly warm.

PER SERVING (5 APPLE CHIPS): CALORIES: 61; TOTAL FAT: 0G; TOTAL CARBS: 16G; FIBER: 3G; SUGAR: 12G; PROTEIN: 0G; SODIUM: 2MG

BAKED SWEET POTATO LATKES

Prep time: 25 minutes • **Cook time:** 20 minutes

Potato latkes (pancakes) are a traditional food for Hanukkah, but their earliest roots are surprisingly in Italy, where the pancakes were made with ricotta cheese. In the early 1300s, an Italian rabbi included these pancakes in a list of dishes to be served for a Purim feast. The idea moved around Europe, with changes along the way. In the 1800s, the form we're familiar with today gained popularity in Eastern Europe as a result of a mass planting of potatoes following crop failures. Traditional latkes are fried, but these are baked to be healthier. Make small latkes for an appetizer and larger ones for a meal. **MAKES 12 TO 14 LARGE LATKES**

Nut-free

1 tablespoon cooking oil

2 medium sweet potatoes, peeled and shredded

⅓ cup chopped scallions, white and green parts

¼ cup all-purpose flour

1 large egg, beaten

½ teaspoon kosher salt

½ teaspoon smoked paprika

¼ teaspoon freshly ground black pepper

OPTIONAL TOPPINGS

Applesauce

Sour cream or plain Greek yogurt

1. Preheat oven to 400°F. Grease a baking sheet with the oil.

2. Combine the sweet potatoes, scallions, flour, egg, salt, paprika, and pepper in a large bowl.

3. Scoop ¼ cup of the sweet potato mixture and place on the baking sheet. Press down to slightly flatten. Repeat with the remaining mixture.

4. Bake for 10 minutes, flip, and continue baking for 5 to 10 minutes more, until the latkes are golden brown. Don't be concerned if the edges brown more deeply and begin to crisp.

5. Remove from the oven and serve with applesauce and/or sour cream (if using).

PER SERVING (3 LATKES): CALORIES: 135; TOTAL FAT: 5G; TOTAL CARBS: 20G; FIBER: 2G; SUGAR: 3G; PROTEIN: 4G; SODIUM: 345MG

HUEVOS RANCHEROS POTATO SKINS

Prep time: 20 minutes • **Cook time:** 25 minutes

I hate wasting food, but luckily white potatoes play well with many other foods. Here are some ideas for using the potato flesh you'll scoop out of the skins for this recipe: mash with a little olive oil and enjoy as a side dish, save and add to your next batch of hash browns, or add to a vegetable soup or casserole. **SERVES 6**

Gluten-free • Nut-free

3 large russet potatoes

2 tablespoons olive oil

½ teaspoon kosher salt

¼ teaspoon freshly ground black pepper

1½ cups grated Mexican cheese mix

1 (15-ounce) can black beans, drained and rinsed

6 large eggs

Salsa (optional)

Avocado chunks (optional)

1. Preheat the oven to 350°F.

2. Pierce the potatoes all over with a fork and microwave on high for 12 minutes, or until softened and cooked through.

3. Halve each potato lengthwise and use a spoon to scoop out the potato flesh, leaving a ½-inch rim of potato intact around the edges and bottoms.

4. Brush the potatoes all over, both the outside skin and the scooped-out interior, with the olive oil and season generously with the salt and pepper. Place the potatoes cut-side up on a baking sheet. Layer the cheese in the bottom of each potato boat, followed by the black beans, leaving enough room for an egg.

5. Crack an egg into each potato half. It's fine if the whites run over a bit, as long as the yolks stay in place.

6. Bake the potatoes until the whites firm up and the yolks are still soft, 15 to 20 minutes, depending on how soft you prefer the yolks. Remove the potatoes from the oven and top with salsa or avocado chunks (if using).

PER SERVING: CALORIES: 405; TOTAL FAT: 17G; TOTAL CARBS: 44G; FIBER: 9G; SUGAR: 3G; PROTEIN: 21G; SODIUM: 515MG

CHEDDAR AND BROCCOLI-STUFFED SWEET POTATOES

Prep time: 15 minutes • **Cook time:** 1 hour 15 minutes

These stuffed sweet potatoes come from a recent vacation to Yellowstone National Park. Much to my surprise, Carnivorous Maximus (my husband) ordered this stuffed potato three nights in row, but it was only available on the third night. Carnivorous Maximus ate every bite and said the wait was worth it. Right then and there, I knew it would find a way into this cookbook. **SERVES 4**

Gluten-free • Nut-free

2 medium sweet potatoes

1 cup broccoli florets, chopped

2 tablespoons thinly sliced scallions, white and green parts

1 (15-ounce) can black beans, drained and rinsed

1 tablespoon unsalted butter

½ cup grated Cheddar cheese, divided

½ teaspoon kosher salt

¼ teaspoon freshly ground black pepper

1. Preheat the oven to 400°F.

2. Prick the sweet potatoes all over with a fork. Place on a baking sheet and bake for 45 to 50 minutes, or until fork tender. (Alternatively, microwave the sweet potatoes on high for 6 to 8 minutes, or until tender.) Leave the oven on.

3. Halve the sweet potatoes lengthwise and let cool slightly. Scoop out the flesh of the potatoes into a small bowl, leaving at least a ¼-inch border around the potato skins.

4. Place a steam insert in a small pot along with 2 inches of water and bring to a boil. Add the broccoli to the pot, cover, and steam until tender, about 5 minutes.

5. Add the steamed broccoli, scallions, black beans, and butter to the bowl with the scooped-out sweet potato flesh. Stir to combine and melt the butter. Stir in ¼ cup of cheese, followed by the salt and pepper.

6. Fill the potato skins with the sweet potato mixture and top with the remaining ¼ cup of cheese. Reduce the oven temperature to 350°F. Place the stuffed sweet potatoes on the baking sheet and bake for 15 minutes.

COOKING TIP: If you roast the potatoes, you can roast the broccoli and scallions on the same baking sheet. Toss the broccoli and scallions in olive oil, sprinkle with salt and pepper, and arrange in a single layer on the baking sheet.

PER SERVING: CALORIES: 295; TOTAL FAT: 8G; TOTAL CARBS: 45G; FIBER: 10G; SUGAR: 18G; PROTEIN: 12G; SODIUM: 430MG

CARAMELIZED MUSHROOMS OVER POLENTA

Prep time: 10 minutes • **Cook time:** 25 minutes

The secret to this dish is cooking the mushrooms and onion long enough for them to caramelize. It takes time, but it's so worth it. You'll want to eat them all before they make it onto the plate with the polenta. The polenta brings a perfect marriage of flavors with the caramelized mushrooms, and any leftover polenta can be used to make fries, croutons for salads, or lasagna layers in place of noodles. **SERVES 2**

Gluten-free: Use gluten-free tamari

½ (18-ounce) tube cooked polenta

5 tablespoons unsalted butter, cut into 1-tablespoon pats, divided

1 yellow onion, finely diced

8 ounces cremini or white mushrooms, thinly sliced

¼ teaspoon kosher salt

2 tablespoons tamari or low-sodium soy sauce

2 tablespoons heavy (whipping) cream

1. Preheat the oven to 200°F.

2. Cut the polenta into 6 (1-inch) slices.

3. Heat 1 tablespoon of butter in a medium skillet over medium-high heat. Add the polenta slices and cook for 3 to 4 minutes, or until golden brown. Flip and cook for another 3 minutes. Transfer to a baking sheet, and put in the oven to keep warm.

4. In the same skillet, melt 2 tablespoons of butter over medium heat. Add the onion, mushrooms, and salt, and sauté until the vegetables begin to caramelize, about 20 minutes. Move the mushroom mixture around occasionally while it cooks, but not too much. Mushrooms give off a lot of liquid, so be sure to continue to cook until the pan is rather dry and the onion and mushrooms begin to crisp.

5. Using a wooden spoon, stir in the remaining 2 tablespoons of butter, followed by the tamari and cream. Cook until a slightly thickened sauce forms, about 2 minutes.

6. Divide the polenta slices between two shallow bowls and top with the mushrooms. Serve warm.

COOKING TIP: Save 10 minutes of cooking time by cooking the polenta and mushrooms at the same time in two separate skillets.

PER SERVING: CALORIES: 542; TOTAL FAT: 35G; TOTAL CARBS: 49G; FIBER: 6G; SUGAR: 7G; PROTEIN: 12G; SODIUM: 1876MG

GARLIC AND PARMESAN SPAGHETTI SQUASH

Prep time: 10 minutes • **Cook time:** 1 hour 15 minutes

Cooking spaghetti squash whole avoids the struggle of cutting through its tough skin, although keeping it whole extends the roasting time in the oven. A great way to avoid that extra cook time is to use an electric pressure cooker like the Instant Pot. Just add 1 cup of water to the pot, then set the spaghetti squash on a trivet inside the pot. Close the lid, select manual, and cook on high pressure for 25 minutes. When the cooking is complete, quick release the pressure. **SERVES 4**

Gluten-free • Nut-free

1 (2- to 3-pound) spaghetti squash

2 tablespoons unsalted butter

2 teaspoons garlic paste or 4 garlic cloves, minced

2 tablespoons chopped fresh Italian parsley

⅓ cup grated Parmesan or Asiago cheese

½ teaspoon kosher salt

¼ teaspoon freshly ground black pepper

¼ cup Roasted Pumpkin Seeds (page 170) or store-bought

1. Preheat the oven to 375°F.

2. Pierce the squash several times with a knife to allow steam to escape during cooking. Put on a baking sheet and roast for 1 hour, or until the squash can be easily pierced with a sharp knife. Let cool for 10 minutes before handling.

3. Slice the squash in half lengthwise and scrape out the seeds with a spoon. Using the tines of a fork, gently scrape the flesh to create long "pasta" strands. If the flesh is still a little hard, just return the squash to the baking sheet, cut-side down, and bake until the flesh is tender. Scrape out all of the pasta strands into a medium bowl.

4. Melt the butter in a large skillet over medium heat. Add the garlic and sauté until fragrant, about 2 minutes. Add the parsley, cheese, salt, pepper, and spaghetti squash. Carefully toss to coat. Cook for 1 to 2 more minutes.

5. Transfer to a serving plate and top with the pumpkin seeds.

PER SERVING: CALORIES: 225; TOTAL FAT: 12G; TOTAL CARBS: 27G; FIBER: 0G; SUGAR: 0G; PROTEIN: 8G; SODIUM: 523MG

How to Roast Squash

Whether you roast a sugar pie pumpkin, butternut squash, acorn squash, or other winter squash, the method is generally the same. As a rule of thumb, if you cook the squash whole, it will take 15 to 20 minutes longer than roasting it halved. The smaller the squash pieces, the shorter the roasting time.

To roast a squash whole

1. Preheat the oven to 400°F.

2. Place the squash on a rimmed baking sheet. Pierce it several times with a sharp knife to allow steam to escape.

3. Roast for about 1 hour, until the squash is tender when pierced with a sharp knife.

To roast squash halves

1. Cut the squash in half by placing a damp towel on a cutting board and placing the squash on top of the towel. The damp towel helps prevent squash with thicker skins from slipping. This extra step isn't necessary for thin-skinned squash.

2. Cut the squash in half lengthwise using a sharp chef's knife.

3. Scrape out the seeds and pulp with a metal spoon, lightly oil the cut surfaces, and place the halves cut-side down on a baking sheet.

4. Roast for about 40 minutes, or until the squash halves are tender when pierced with a sharp knife.

To roast squash seeds

1. Remove the seeds from the pulp. This can be tricky, but the payoff is worth it. Place the pulp with the seeds in a bowl of water, and separate the seeds from the pulp with your fingers. Spread them on a paper towel to dry overnight before roasting.

2. Preheat your oven to 350°F.

3. On a parchment-lined baking sheet, sprinkle the seeds in an even layer, making sure they don't overlap so they will cook evenly. Sprinkle with the seasoning of your choice. Roast for 15 minutes, then stir them. Roast for another 10 minutes, or until the seeds are golden brown; make sure the seasoning doesn't burn, or else the seeds will taste bitter.

4. Eat the seeds whole, husk and all, for extra fiber and crunch!

ROASTED BROCCOLI BOWL WITH AN EGG

Prep time: 15 minutes · **Cook time:** 30 minutes

This bowl of deliciousness has an egg fried "over easy" placed on top right before serving. The "over" indicates the egg is flipped over once the whites firm up on the bottom, and the "easy" means the yolk still runs easily when broken. If you prefer your eggs "over medium" or "over hard," just cook the second side a little longer. Eggs sunny-side up are also fried, but they're never flipped. Instead the egg whites on top are barely cooked, and the yolk is always runny. It's common to cover the pan to ensure the whites are cooked. **SERVES 2**

Nut-free
Dairy-free: Use olive oil for the butter and vegan mozzarella for the Parmesan

2½ cups water or vegetable broth

½ cup semi-pearled farro

1½ teaspoons kosher salt, divided

1 bunch broccoli (about 1½ pounds)

3 tablespoons olive oil, divided

¼ teaspoon freshly ground black pepper

2 tablespoons freshly squeezed lemon juice

⅓ cup coarsely grated Parmesan cheese

½ tablespoon unsalted butter

2 large eggs

1. Preheat the oven to 450°F. Line a rimmed baking sheet with parchment paper.

2. Bring the water to a boil in a small pot over high heat. Add the farro with 1 teaspoon of salt. Reduce the heat to a simmer, cover, and cook until al dente, about 30 minutes. Drain any excess liquid and transfer to a large bowl.

3. Trim the ends of the broccoli and slice the stems ½ inch thick on the diagonal. Cut the florets into bite-size pieces. Arrange on the prepared baking sheet in a single layer, drizzle with 1 tablespoon of olive oil, and season with the black pepper and remaining ½ teaspoon of salt. Roast for about 15 minutes, until the florets are browned around the edges.

4. Transfer the florets to the bowl with the farro, and, if necessary, continue to roast the stems until tender. The total roasting time will depend on the size of the stems.

5. Place the stems in the bowl with the florets and farro. Toss with the remaining 2 tablespoons of olive oil, the lemon juice, and cheese.

6. Melt the butter in a small nonstick skillet over medium heat. Break the eggs into the skillet and fry until the whites just turn opaque and firm up. Flip and cook for no more than 10 seconds for runny yolks.

7. Divide the farro-broccoli mixture between two bowls or plates and top each with a fried egg.

PREP TIP: If you have frozen cooked farro on hand, this dish comes together with much less fuss and time. Just add the farro to the baking sheet with the broccoli, with a drizzle of olive oil.

FLEXITARIAN TIP: Cooked chorizo, with its spicy, salty flavor, is a great addition to this bowl.

PER SERVING: CALORIES: 523; TOTAL FAT: 36G; TOTAL CARBS: 32G; FIBER: 10G; SUGAR: 7G; PROTEIN: 27G; SODIUM: 1987MG

LENTIL POTATO SALAD

Prep time: 10 minutes · **Cook time:** 25 minutes

Tiny, black, and round, beluga lentils are named for the caviar they resemble. In addition to their striking appearance, beluga lentils have a mild flavor and hold their shape well during cooking, unlike some other lentils that tend to become mushy. All of this makes them perfect for salads like this one. **SERVES 2**

Dairy-free · **Gluten-free** · **Nut-free** · **Vegan**

½ cup beluga lentils

8 fingerling potatoes

1 cup thinly sliced scallions

¼ cup halved cherry tomatoes

¼ cup Lemon Vinaigrette (page 15)

Kosher salt, to taste

Freshly ground black pepper, to taste

1. Bring 2 cups of water to a simmer in a small pot and add the lentils. Cover and simmer for 20 to 25 minutes, or until the lentils are tender. Drain and set aside to cool.

2. While the lentils are cooking, bring a medium pot of well-salted water to a boil and add the potatoes. Reduce the heat to a simmer and cook for about 15 minutes, or until the potatoes are tender. Drain. Once cool enough to handle, slice or halve the potatoes.

3. Place the lentils on a serving plate and top with the potatoes, scallions, and tomatoes. Drizzle with the vinaigrette and season with the salt and pepper.

PREP TIP: Be careful to keep the lentils cooking at a steady, low simmer. They risk splitting when cooked in rapidly boiling water.

PER SERVING: CALORIES: 400; TOTAL FAT: 26G; TOTAL CARBS: 39G; FIBER: 6G; SUGAR: 5G; PROTEIN: 7G; SODIUM: 1200MG

WARM GRAIN SALAD WITH MISO BUTTER

Prep time: 15 minutes • **Cook time:** 30 minutes

Farro, an ancient wheat, touts a high protein and fiber content and has a nutty, chewy texture that makes it great for grain salads and soups. It's sold whole, semi-pearled, or pearled, any of which can be used for this recipe. The difference between the types lies in their cooking time and their nutritional content, with whole farro being the most nutritious and pearled the least. **SERVES 4**

Nut-free

2½ cups water or
vegetable broth

1 cup semi-pearled uncooked
farro or 3 cups cooked

1 teaspoon kosher salt, divided

1 pound green beans, trimmed
and cut into 2-inch pieces

2 cups halved cherry tomatoes

1 small red onion, sliced into
½-inch wedges

1 to 2 teaspoons olive oil

½ teaspoon freshly ground
black pepper

¼ cup Miso Butter (page 174),
at room temperature

1. Preheat the oven to 400°F.

2. Bring the water or broth to a boil in a small pot over medium-high heat. Add the farro and ½ teaspoon of salt. Reduce the heat to a simmer, cover, and cook for 30 minutes, or until al dente. (If using cooked farro, skip this step.)

3. Place the green beans, tomatoes, and onion wedges on a rimmed baking sheet. Drizzle with the olive oil and toss to coat. Spread into a single layer and sprinkle evenly with the black pepper and remaining ½ teaspoon of salt. Roast until the beans and onions are tender and very lightly crisped, about 15 minutes.

4. When the vegetables are roasted, toss them with the farro and miso butter right on the baking pan. The heat of the pan and vegetables will melt the butter.

5. Serve warm.

COOKING TIP: Tofu is a great addition to this dish. Slice pieces of tofu from a block, and gently press to release as much water as possible. Roast the tofu on the baking sheet with the vegetables.

PER SERVING: CALORIES: 182; TOTAL FAT: 9G; TOTAL CARBS: 23G; FIBER: 7G; SUGAR: 6G; PROTEIN: 6G; SODIUM: 961MG

LEMONY KALE, AVOCADO, AND CHICKPEA SALAD

Prep time: 20 minutes

Kale is one of the tougher winter greens, and it benefits from a deep tissue massage. But did you know that massaged kale is also better for you? Raw kale can be difficult for your stomach to break down. Massaging the leaves essentially breaks down fibers of the kale, making it easier to digest. Most recipes call for massaging the leaves with lemon juice and salt, but this recipe adds mashed avocado to create a creamy dressing. **SERVES 4**

Gluten-free • Nut-free • Vegan

1 avocado, halved

2 tablespoons freshly squeezed lemon juice, divided

½ teaspoon kosher salt, divided

1 bunch curly kale, stems removed and discarded, leaves coarsely chopped (about 8 cups)

1 (15-ounce) can chickpeas, drained and rinsed

2 tablespoons extra-virgin olive oil

¼ teaspoon freshly ground black pepper

¼ cup Roasted Pumpkin Seeds (page 170) or store-bought

1. Scoop the flesh from one of the avocado halves out of its skin and put it in a large bowl. Add 1 tablespoon of lemon juice and ¼ teaspoon of salt, and mash everything together. Add the coarsely chopped kale leaves and massage them by hand with the avocado mash until the kale becomes tender. Place the kale-avocado mash on a serving plate.

2. Remove the flesh of the remaining avocado half from its skin and chop into bite-size chunks. Place in the bowl that contained the kale, and add the chickpeas.

3. In a small bowl, whisk together the olive oil, remaining 1 tablespoon of lemon juice, remaining ¼ teaspoon of salt, and the pepper. Drizzle over the chickpeas and avocado and toss to combine. Pile on top of the kale-avocado mash, and top with the roasted pumpkin seeds.

FLEXITARIAN TIP: Add roasted chicken to the salad.

PER SERVING: CALORIES: 383; TOTAL FAT: 20G; TOTAL CARBS: 43G; FIBER: 12G; SUGAR: 4G; PROTEIN: 14G; SODIUM: 360MG

ROASTED CAULIFLOWER AND
RICE BOWL WITH TOMATOES

Prep time: 10 minutes • **Cook time:** 45 minutes

The difference between brown and white rice is that the bran and germ layers are left intact in brown rice, giving the rice a nutty, grainy flavor and a chewy bite. The most common types of long-grain brown rice found in markets are basmati, an extra-long, nutty rice popular in Indian cuisine, and jasmine, a slightly floral, softer rice used in many Asian dishes. I typically use basmati, but feel free to use whichever rice you prefer in this dish. **SERVES 4**

Dairy-free • Gluten-free • Nut-free • Vegan

1 cup long-grain brown rice

2 cups water or vegetable broth

2 teaspoons kosher salt, divided

4 large shallots, quartered

4 Roma tomatoes, halved
    lengthwise

1 small cauliflower, cut
    into bite-size chunks,
    or 1 (16-ounce) bag
    frozen florets

¼ cup olive oil

½ teaspoon freshly ground
    black pepper

2 tablespoons balsamic vinegar

1. Preheat the oven to 400°F. Line a rimmed baking sheet with parchment paper.

2. Rinse the rice under cool water and drain. Bring the water and 1 teaspoon of salt to a boil in a medium pot over medium-high heat. Add the rice, reduce the heat to a simmer, and cover. Cook, covered, for 45 minutes, or until tender. Fluff the cooked rice with a fork and set aside.

3. While the rice is cooking, arrange the shallots, tomatoes (cut-sides facing up), and cauliflower on the prepared baking sheet. Drizzle with the olive oil and toss to coat. Sprinkle everything with the remaining 1 teaspoon of salt and the pepper.

4. Roast until the cauliflower and shallots are tender and the edges just begin to crisp, about 30 minutes.

5. Divide the brown rice between bowls and top with the roasted vegetables. Drizzle each serving with the balsamic vinegar.

INGREDIENT TIP: If you don't follow a vegan diet, add a fried or soft-boiled egg on top.

PER SERVING: CALORIES: 220; TOTAL FAT: 13G; TOTAL CARBS: 24G; FIBER: 6G; SUGAR: 7G; PROTEIN: 5G; SODIUM: 1214MG

TOMATO GALETTES

Prep time: 20 minutes • **Cook time:** 25 minutes

Galettes are a crowd pleaser, and easy to make. Just thaw and roll out store-bought dough, layer vegetables in the middle, and fold and pleat the crust up around them. The biggest drawback of a galette is that the crust can't be pre-baked, and sometimes results in a slightly soggy bottom. For that reason, I use Roma tomatoes because they aren't as wet as juicy, in-season tomatoes. Other techniques for preventing soggy galettes are to bake them on a pizza stone, baste the bottom with egg white, or add a sprinkling of bread-crumbs on the pastry before layering the food on top. **SERVES 2**

Nut-free

1 frozen store-bought pastry round, thawed and formed into a 13-inch round

5 or 6 ripe Roma tomatoes, sliced crosswise ¼ inch thick

½ teaspoon kosher salt, divided

¼ teaspoon freshly ground black pepper, divided

⅔ cup shredded mozzarella cheese

⅓ cup mayonnaise

¼ cup finely chopped fresh herbs, such as basil, parsley, and/or oregano

1. Preheat the oven to 425°F. Position a rack in the center of the oven. Place a pizza stone or baking sheet turned upside down on the rack while the oven preheats.

2. Place the pastry round on a sheet of parchment paper on the counter.

3. Arrange the tomato slices in two circles starting from the middle of the pastry, slightly overlapping the tomatoes. Be sure to leave a minimum 1½-inch border around the outer edge of the dough. Sprinkle the tomatoes with ¼ teaspoon of salt and ⅛ teaspoon of black pepper.

4. In a small bowl, combine the mozzarella, mayonnaise, herbs, remaining ¼ teaspoon of salt, and remaining ⅛ teaspoon of black pepper. Place dollops of the cheese mixture over the tomatoes.

5. Fold the excess dough over the tomatoes to form a crust border. Transfer the galette on the parchment paper to the preheated pizza stone or baking sheet. Bake for 20 to 25 minutes, or until the crust is golden and the cheese is melted and bubbling.

6. Remove from the oven and let cool for 15 minutes before cutting.

SUBSTITUTION TIP: In fall, make this galette with butternut squash, kale, and manchego cheese, or try one with broccoli and cauliflower topped with Cheddar. For a Thanksgiving dessert, toss apple slices with butter, sugar, and cinnamon, and fold the pastry up around them.

PER SERVING: CALORIES: 419; TOTAL FAT: 30G; TOTAL CARBS: 27G; FIBER: 4G; SUGAR: 9G; PROTEIN: 12G; SODIUM: 1155MG

TACO PIZZAS WITH REFRIED BEANS

Prep time: 15 minutes • **Cook time:** 20 minutes

Pizza crust is personal. Some people like it thin and crispy, while others prefer it thick and soft. Not all store-bought pizza crusts are created equally, and it's only by experimenting with a few that you'll find your favorite. Choose your own path with the crust, or do what I do and just use naan flatbread. **SERVES 2**

Nut-free

2 large naan flatbread or 2 (12-inch) store-bought pizza crusts

1 (16-ounce) can refried beans

8 to 10 tortilla chips, lightly crumbled

4 large Roma tomatoes, finely diced

2 (8-ounce) packages grated Mexican cheese mix

OPTIONAL TOPPINGS

Sour cream

Pickled jalapeño pepper rings

Guacamole

1. Preheat the oven to 450°F. Place a rack in the center of the oven and put a pizza stone or a baking sheet turned upside down on the rack while the oven heats.

2. Bake the naan on the pizza stone or upturned baking sheet until lightly toasted, about 5 minutes. If using store-bought pizza rusts, follow the directions on the package to bake 2 pizza crusts.

3. Divide the refried beans, tortilla chips, tomatoes, and cheese between the two flatbreads. Bake for 10 to 15 minutes, or until the cheese is melted.

4. Slice each pizza into 8 pieces and serve with your preferred toppings as desired.

PER SERVING: CALORIES: 1346; TOTAL FAT: 81G; TOTAL CARBS: 87G; FIBER: 15G; SUGAR: 5G; PROTEIN: 68G; SODIUM: 2643MG

OPEN-FACE MEDITERRANEAN EGG SALAD

Prep time: 10 minutes • **Cook time:** 12 minutes

Whenever I bring home a dozen eggs, I often take a few out to hard boil. Once they're cooked, I pencil them with an "H" and slip them back into the egg carton. Having them on hand makes them easy to add to salads and roasted vegetables for a little extra protein, or to peel for an on-the-run breakfast. If you have hard-boiled eggs all ready to go, this little dish comes together in about 10 minutes. **SERVES 2**

Dairy-free • **Nut-free**
Gluten-free: Use gluten-free bread

2 tablespoons store-bought basil pesto

2 slices whole-wheat bread, toasted

3 hard-boiled eggs

1 tablespoon mayonnaise

½ avocado, sliced lengthwise

2 tablespoons extra-virgin olive oil

1. Spread the pesto on both slices of toasted bread and set aside.

2. Coarsely chop the eggs and place in a small bowl. Add the mayonnaise and mix to combine.

3. Divide the egg and mayo mixture between the toasts, top with the avocado slices, and finish with a drizzle of olive oil.

PER SERVING: CALORIES: 460; TOTAL FAT: 37G; TOTAL CARBS: 20G; FIBER: 6G; SUGAR: 4G; PROTEIN: 15G; SODIUM: 389MG

DELICATA SQUASH AND BLACK BEAN QUESADILLAS

Prep time: 15 minutes • **Cook time:** 30 to 35 minutes

One of my favorite things about Delicata squash is that it doesn't need to be peeled. The skin is thin enough that the squash can be seeded, roasted, and eaten whole. But if you want to speed this recipe along, substitute frozen diced butternut squash. Add it to the skillet with the black beans chili powder, salt, and pepper, and divide among the tortillas with the cheese. **SERVES 4**

Nut-free

1 small Delicata squash, halved lengthwise, seeded, and cut crosswise into ¼-inch slices

3 teaspoons olive oil, divided

½ teaspoon kosher salt

¼ teaspoon freshly ground black pepper

8 (8-inch) flour tortillas

1 (15-ounce) can black beans, drained and rinsed

1 teaspoon chili powder

2 cups grated pepper jack cheese

OPTIONAL TOPPINGS

Sour cream

Guacamole

Pickled jalapeño pepper rings

Cilantro

Diced tomatoes

1. Preheat the oven to 425°F. Line a baking sheet with parchment paper.

2. Arrange the half-moon slices of squash on the baking sheet and drizzle with 2 teaspoons of olive oil. Sprinkle lightly with the salt and pepper and toss to coat. Roast until tender, about 20 minutes. Remove from the oven, but keep the oven on. Slide the parchment paper and the squash off the baking sheet, and line the baking sheet with another sheet of parchment paper.

3. Place 4 flour tortillas on the baking sheet. Divide the black beans among the tortillas, add the chili powder, and lightly mash using a fork. Sprinkle ½ cup of cheese across the 4 tortillas, and divide the roasted squash among them. Top with another ½ cup of cheese. Place a tortilla on top of each of the stacks and press down slightly. Lightly baste the tortilla tops with the remaining 1 teaspoon of olive oil.

4. Bake until golden brown and the cheese is melted, about 10 to 12 minutes. Transfer to a plate.

5. Cut into wedges and add toppings as desired.

FLEXITARIAN TIP: Add shredded roast chicken to the quesadilla.

PER SERVING: CALORIES: 620; TOTAL FAT: 27G; TOTAL CARBS: 68G; FIBER: 11G; SUGAR: 2G; PROTEIN: 26G; SODIUM: 1084MG

GRILLED FONTINA SANDWICHES WITH RED PEPPERS

Prep time: 10 minutes • **Cook time:** 7 minutes

Fontina is a semisoft cow's-milk cheese produced in northern Italy that has a buttery, nutty flavor. It is also a great melting cheese. If you don't have easy access to this cheese, most melty cheeses, such as Cheddar, Jack, pepper jack, and Swiss, will work fine in this sandwich. Or try a combination of cheeses for more depth of flavor. **SERVES 2**

Nut-free
Gluten-free: Use gluten-free bread

4 slices white sandwich bread

1 tablespoon Dijon mustard

4 ounces fontina cheese, thinly sliced

2 tablespoons Easy Roasted Red Pepper Aioli (page 177) or 1 medium jarred roasted red peppers, drained, dried, and thinly sliced

1 cup baby arugula

4 tablespoons unsalted butter, at room temperature, divided

1. Place 2 slices of bread on a flat surface and spread the mustard on each. Divide half of the fontina cheese between the slices, and layer the red pepper aioli and arugula on top of the cheese. Top the arugula with the remaining fontina. Close the sandwiches with the remaining 2 slices of bread.

2. Lightly butter the top slices of bread with 1 tablespoon of butter.

3. Melt 1 tablespoon of butter in a large nonstick skillet over medium heat. Arrange the sandwiches in the skillet butter-side down. Lightly butter the top slices of bread with another 1 tablespoon of butter.

4. Cover and cook until the bread is lightly toasted, 2 to 3 minutes. Carefully flip, adding the remaining 1 tablespoon of butter if needed. Cover the skillet again and cook until the bread is lightly toasted and the cheese is melted, about 2 minutes.

FLEXITARIAN TIP: Add a few slices of prosciutto to each sandwich.

PER SERVING: CALORIES: 499; TOTAL FAT: 42G; TOTAL CARBS: 15G; FIBER: 2G; SUGAR: 5G; PROTEIN: 17G; SODIUM: 833MG

CAPRESE AVOCADO GRILLED PITAS

Prep time: 10 minutes • **Cook time:** 10 minutes

Caprese salad is a classic appetizer enjoyed all through the summer. Originating on the island of Capri, it's one of the easiest dishes to assemble. All you need are slices of mozzarella and tomato, interwoven with fresh basil. The salad is drizzled with olive oil and topped with a dusting of salt and pepper. This easy pita sandwich is a twist on this classic, using basil pesto and adding a little avocado. **SERVES 2**

Nut-free

2 pita rounds

2 tablespoons basil pesto

8 slices mozzarella cheese

1 large, ripe tomato, sliced

1 avocado, sliced lengthwise into wedges

Extra-virgin olive oil, for the grill pan

1. Cut each pita round in half to make 4 pockets. Open each pocket and spread the pesto on both sides.

2. Layer one slice of mozzarella inside each of the 4 pita pockets, top with slices of tomato and avocado, and end with another slice of mozzarella.

3. Heat a grill pan over medium-high heat and add just enough olive oil to lightly slick the surface. Place the pita pockets in the pan and cook for 3 to 4 minutes on each side, or until the cheese is melted.

FLEXITARIAN TIP: Add slices of crisp bacon to the pitas before grilling.

PER SERVING: CALORIES: 524; TOTAL FAT: 40G; TOTAL CARBS: 29G; FIBER: 10G; SUGAR: 4G; PROTEIN: 18G; SODIUM: 511MG

SWISS CHARD PESTO LINGUINE

Prep time: 10 minutes • **Cook time:** 15 minutes

Raw Swiss chard can be bitter, but a brief dip in hot water smooths out the flavor, so don't skip this step. I've found that the best way to remove excess moisture from greens following blanching is to roll them up in a towel and squeeze, but for this recipe, using a spoon to press down on the drenched chard in a colander will suffice. A variation of this dish is to eliminate the chard altogether and create a pesto using the remaining ingredients with ½ cup of sun-dried tomatoes, a handful of fresh basil leaves, and a little red wine vinegar. **SERVES 2**

Nut-free

½ pound linguine

3 cups stemmed and coarsely chopped Swiss chard

½ large shallot, coarsely chopped

⅓ cup grated Parmesan or Asiago cheese

¼ teaspoon kosher salt

¼ teaspoon freshly ground black pepper

¼ cup extra-virgin olive oil

2 tablespoons sliced sun-dried tomatoes

1. Bring a large pot of well-salted water to a boil and cook the pasta according to the package directions. Transfer the pasta to a bowl using tongs or a large perforated spoon, and reserve ¼ cup of pasta water.

2. Return the remaining pasta water in the pot to a boil and add the chopped Swiss chard leaves to the pot. Blanch for 3 minutes, then drain in a colander. Press down on the leaves with a spoon to squeeze out as much water as possible. Transfer to the bowl of a food processor or a small blender.

3. Add the shallot, cheese, salt, pepper, reserved pasta water, and olive oil to the food processor and process into a slightly chunky sauce.

4. Add the sauce and sun-dried tomatoes to the bowl with the pasta and toss to combine.

FLEXITARIAN TIP: Add crumbled bacon strips to the pasta.

PER SERVING: CALORIES: 541; TOTAL FAT: 32G; TOTAL CARBS: 49G; FIBER: 4G; SUGAR: 3G; PROTEIN: 16G; SODIUM: 998MG

EASY ASPARAGUS CARBONARA

Prep time: 15 minutes • **Cook time:** 30 minutes

Carbonara traditionally uses the heat of the pasta to cook the eggs, but there's some risk, although small, that the eggs will not be cooked enough. I always whisk in the eggs over low heat, and recommend using pasteurized eggs, which are sold in a liquid form or in the shell. Safest Choice Eggs sells pasteurized eggs and has a store locator on its website to help you find stores in your area that carry them. I don't recommend this dish for very young children or anyone with a compromised immune system. **SERVES 2**

Nut-free

8 ounces orecchiette pasta

2 tablespoons olive oil

2 cups asparagus, sliced into 2-inch pieces

⅛ teaspoon sea salt

⅛ teaspoon freshly ground black pepper

2 large pasteurized egg yolks, at room temperature

½ cup grated Parmesan cheese

2 tablespoons Lemony Breadcrumbs (page 171)

1. Bring a Dutch oven–type pot of well-salted water to a boil. Cook the pasta according to the package directions. Reserve ½ cup of pasta water, then drain the pasta.

2. In the same pot you used to cook the pasta, and heat the olive oil over medium-high heat. Add the asparagus, salt, and pepper and sauté for 10 minutes, or until the asparagus is lightly browned and just tender.

3. Reduce the heat to low, add the pasta back to the pot, and lightly toss to coat.

4. In a small bowl, whisk together the egg yolks, cheese, and reserved pasta water. Slowly stream the egg mixture over the pasta and asparagus, stirring constantly, until the egg mixture thickens into a glossy sauce and the cheese is melted.

5. Top with breadcrumbs and serve immediately.

PREP TIP: An effective way of quickly bringing eggs to room temperature is to place cold eggs in a bowl of very warm water for 10 minutes.

PER SERVING: CALORIES: 718; TOTAL FAT: 27G; TOTAL CARBS: 94G; FIBER: 7G; SUGAR: 7G; PROTEIN: 30G; SODIUM: 441MG

GARLIC AND CRUSHED RED PEPPER LINGUINE

Prep time: 10 minutes • **Cook time:** 25 minutes

This satisfying dish is known as *spaghetti aglio e olio* in Italy and can be found on many menus, and on many family tables, throughout the country. Italian children are practically raised on it. The garlic component of the dish is critical to its success. The trick is adding the pasta water to the olive oil and garlic once the garlic begins to sizzle. This immediately lowers its temperature and coddles it until it turns a golden brown. Otherwise, garlic becomes quite bitter when cooked at too high a temperature. **SERVES 4**

Nut-free

1 pound spaghetti

¼ cup olive oil

1 tablespoon garlic paste or 1½ tablespoons minced garlic

¼ teaspoon red pepper flakes, or to taste

½ cup finely chopped fresh Italian parsley

½ cup grated Parmesan cheese, divided

Kosher salt, to taste

Freshly ground black pepper, to taste

1. Bring a large pot of lightly salted water to a boil. Cook the spaghetti according to the package directions. Reserve ¼ cup of the pasta water and set aside. Drain the pasta and transfer it to a large bowl.

2. Combine the olive oil and garlic in a skillet over medium heat. Be sure to add the garlic to the oil before it heats up, allowing it to slowly toast and infuse the oil. Cook until the garlic begins to sizzle, about 1 minute. Reduce the heat to medium-low and add 2 tablespoons of the reserved pasta water, the red pepper flakes, and parsley. Add additional pasta water if necessary to create a sauce. Cook on medium-low for another 5 to 10 minutes, until the garlic turns golden. Remove the pan from the heat.

3. Pour the garlic oil over the pasta and toss to coat. Add half the cheese and toss to combine. Season with salt and pepper. Top the pasta with the remaining cheese and serve.

FLEXITARIAN TIP: Add sautéed shrimp to the pasta.

PER SERVING: CALORIES: 369; TOTAL FAT: 17G; TOTAL CARBS: 44G; FIBER: 2G; SUGAR: 2G; PROTEIN: 12G; SODIUM: 139MG

SPAGHETTI SQUASH PASTA WITH BROCCOLINI AND LEMON

Prep time: 10 minutes • **Cook time:** 30 minutes

I feel like I'm taking my life in my hands every time I cut an uncooked spaghetti squash in half. Cooking it whole in the Instant Pot was game-changing. It cooks in 25 minutes flat, giving me just the right amount of time to sauté the other vegetables. If you don't have an Instant Pot or other pressure cooker, you can easily roast the spaghetti squash whole or sliced in half lengthwise. Preheat the oven to 400°F and roast for approximately 1 hour for an intact squash, or 40 minutes for one that's been sliced in half, depending on the size of the squash. A sharp knife should easily puncture the skin and flesh when done. **SERVES 4**

Dairy-free • **Gluten-free** • **Nut-free** • **Vegan**

1 cup water, plus
2 to 3 tablespoons

1 small (2- to 3-pound)
spaghetti squash

2 tablespoons olive oil

4 to 5 cups roughly cut
broccolini, or broccoli florets
and small stalks only

1 tablespoon freshly squeezed
lemon juice

½ teaspoon kosher salt

¼ teaspoon freshly ground
black pepper

⅛ teaspoon smoked paprika

2 tablespoons Roasted Pumpkin
Seeds (page 170) or
store-bought

1. Pour 1 cup of water into the inner cooking pot of an electric pressure cooker. Place the trivet rack on the bottom and set the spaghetti squash on the rack. Trim the ends of the spaghetti squash, if needed, so it will fit.

2. Lock the lid in place. Select manual and cook at high pressure for 25 minutes.

3. When the cooking is complete, quick release the pressure. Unlock the lid and remove the squash to cool.

4. While the spaghetti squash cooks, heat the olive oil in a large skillet over medium heat. Add the broccolini, lemon juice, salt, pepper, and paprika. Toss to coat, and sauté for 15 to 20 minutes. Stir in 2 to 3 tablespoons of water, scraping up any bits of broccolini stuck to the bottom of the skillet. Cover and cook for another 5 to 10 minutes, or until the broccolini is tender.

5. Once the squash is cool enough to handle, slice it in half. Scoop out and discard the seeds and pulp. Lightly scrape the tines of a fork through the squash flesh to pull apart long strands of squash. Pile the strands into a serving bowl.

6. Lightly toss the broccolini into the spaghetti squash and serve with a flurry of the roasted pumpkin seeds.

FLEXITARIAN TIP: Cook up some bacon, sausage, or chorizo in a separate skillet, drain, and add to the dish at the end.

PER SERVING: CALORIES: 179; TOTAL FAT: 9G; TOTAL CARBS: 25G; FIBER: 3G; SUGAR: 2G; PROTEIN: 5G; SODIUM: 368MG

BUTTERMILK CORNBREAD–TOPPED
CHILI (PAGE 118)

5

ONE POT & SKILLET

SPICY SKILLET EGGS

Prep time: 10 minutes • **Cook time:** 30 minutes

This recipe is a twist on a Middle Eastern and North African favorite called *shakshuka*. In Israel, this is breakfast, served with flatbreads or challah on the side. Wherever you have it, it's always a one-skillet meal of eggs poached in a spicy tomato–red pepper sauce. In this version, I add black beans to make it heartier. **SERVES 4**

Gluten-free • **Nut-free**
Dairy-free: Omit the cheese

1 tablespoon olive oil

½ medium yellow onion, diced

1 (15-ounce) can black beans, drained and rinsed

1 red bell pepper, seeded and chopped

1 teaspoon garlic paste or minced garlic

1 teaspoon chili powder

½ teaspoon dried oregano

½ teaspoon red pepper flakes

1 teaspoon kosher salt

1 (28-ounce) can diced tomatoes with their juices

4 large eggs

¼ cup small basil leaves

½ avocado, chopped (optional)

1. Heat the olive oil in a large skillet over medium-high heat. Add the onion, beans, bell pepper, garlic, chili powder, oregano, red pepper flakes, and salt. Sauté until the onion and bell pepper are soft, about 10 minutes.

2. Add the tomatoes and cook for about 10 minutes until they begin to gently simmer.

3. Form four hollows into the mixture with a large spoon. Break one egg into a small bowl, then slide it into one of the hollows without breaking the yolk. Repeat with the other three eggs.

4. Cover the pan, reduce the heat to medium-low, and gently simmer for 10 minutes, or until the egg whites firm up but the yolks remain runny.

5. Serve topped with the basil leaves and avocado (if using).

PER SERVING: CALORIES: 367; TOTAL FAT: 19G; TOTAL CARBS: 33G; FIBER: 12G; SUGAR: 3G; PROTEIN: 20G; SODIUM: 867MG

VEGGIE HASH WITH POACHED EGGS

Prep time: 10 minutes • **Cook time:** 20 minutes

I call this breakfast-for-dinner, although it can be served any time of day. You can cook this dish in a nonstick pan to make flipping the eggs easier, but I find a thin metal spatula is all I need with my well-seasoned cast iron skillet. Heating oil in an already hot skillet of any kind helps to prevent food sticking to the pan, and if the oil heats up a bit before adding the food, it's almost foolproof for even fried eggs. **SERVES 4**

Gluten-free • Nut-free

1 tablespoon unsalted butter

2 cups thinly sliced
    Brussels sprouts

1 large white russet potato,
    peeled and finely diced
    (about 2 cups)

1 cup thinly sliced leeks or onions

½ teaspoon kosher salt

¼ teaspoon freshly ground
    black pepper

½ cup vegetable broth

2 tablespoons olive oil

4 large eggs

1. Melt the butter in a large skillet and add the Brussels sprouts, potato, leeks, salt, and pepper. Sauté until the vegetables are browned, about 10 minutes.

2. Add the vegetable broth and simmer until the liquid is absorbed and the vegetables are tender, about 5 minutes.

3. Lay out 4 plates and transfer ¼ of the vegtables to each plate. Set aside.

4. Add the olive oil to the skillet. Break the eggs into a bowl. (I like to break them first into a bowl to ensure the yolks aren't broken before they hit the pan.) When the oil is hot, slide the eggs, one by one, into the skillet, as it's easier to flip eggs that have been added individually. Fry the eggs until the whites become opaque and start to firm up. Flip and cook for no more than 10 seconds for a runny yolk.

5. On each of the 4 plates, top the hash with an egg.

SUBSTITUTION TIP: If your house is a no–Brussels sprouts zone, you can substitute chopped broccoli with great success.

PER SERVING: CALORIES: 266; TOTAL FAT: 15G; TOTAL CARBS: 24G; FIBER: 4G; SUGAR: 3G; PROTEIN: 11G; SODIUM: 498MG

ASPARAGUS FRITTATA

Prep time: 5 minutes • **Cook time:** 15 minutes

Frittatas are the perfect weekend breakfast when you have houseguests. They don't require a lot of planning, you can use whatever you have in the refrigerator, and your guests will be impressed and eat every bite. This springtime version highlights asparagus and leek, but other winning combinations include mushrooms and baby spinach leaves, or Balsamic Roasted Tomatoes (page 168) with steamed broccoli. **SERVES 4**

Gluten-free • Nut-free

2 tablespoons unsalted butter

1 small leek, white and very light green parts only, thinly sliced

2 cups chopped asparagus

¼ teaspoon dried thyme

6 large eggs

½ cup part-skim ricotta cheese

1 teaspoon kosher salt

½ teaspoon freshly ground black pepper

¼ cup grated Parmesan cheese

1. Melt the butter in a nonstick ovenproof pan over medium heat. Add the leek and sauté for about 3 minutes, or until it just starts to become tender. Add the asparagus and thyme. Sauté until the asparagus is tender, about 5 minutes, depending on the thickness of the spears.

2. Preheat the broiler.

3. In a medium bowl, whisk together the eggs, ricotta cheese, salt, and pepper. Pour into the pan with the asparagus and leek, and move the vegetables around to make sure they're evenly distributed. Cover and cook for 3 minutes, or until the sides of the frittata firm up.

4. Uncover the frittata and spread the Parmesan cheese across the top. Slide the pan under the broiler and broil for 2 to 3 minutes, or until the cheese is melted and the frittata feels firm to the touch.

COOKING TIP: If you cut the recipe in half, it will only require 1 minute under the broiler.

PER SERVING: CALORIES: 250; TOTAL FAT: 7G; TOTAL CARBS: 8G; FIBER: 3G; SUGAR: 2G; PROTEIN: 17G; SODIUM: 796MG

SKILLET POTATOES WITH SWISS CHARD AND ONION

Prep time: 20 minutes • **Cook time:** 40 minutes

This is one of my go-to comfort meals at the end of a long day, and it invites many substitutions. Most greens can stand in for the Swiss chard, including spinach, kale, and mustard greens. If you don't have potatoes on hand, substitute a cup or more of cooked quinoa, and add a few capers and sliced green olives if you want a touch of salty umami. For an extra punch of protein (and if you are not feeding a vegan), create two little indentations in the onions and chard once they're layered on the potatoes. Crack an egg in each. Cover the skillet and cook until the whites firm up and the yolks are still runny. **SERVES 2**

Dairy-free • Gluten-free • Nut-free • Vegan

1 bunch Swiss chard (about 4 cups when chopped)

2 tablespoons olive oil, divided

1 yellow onion, diced

¾ teaspoon kosher salt, divided

¾ teaspoon freshly ground black pepper, divided

2 tablespoons freshly squeezed lemon juice

1½ pounds white russet potatoes, peeled and diced

¼ cup vegetable broth

1. Remove the leaves of the Swiss chard from the central stems. Discard the stems. Stack the leaves and slice horizontally into 2-inch wide pieces. Wash and drain well.

2. Heat 1 tablespoon of olive oil in a medium nonstick skillet over medium-high heat. Add the onion, ¼ teaspoon of salt, and ¼ teaspoon of pepper, and cook until softened, about 10 minutes.

3. Add the Swiss chard and lemon juice. Toss and cook until the leaves are wilted, about 3 minutes. Transfer the onion and chard to a bowl.

4. Add the remaining 1 tablespoon of olive oil to the skillet, along with the potatoes, remaining ½ teaspoon of salt, and remaining ½ teaspoon of pepper. Cook the potatoes until they just start to brown a bit, tossing a few times, about 5 minutes. Add the broth and cook on a low simmer for 10 minutes, or until the liquid is absorbed and the potatoes are tender. Add the onion and chard on top and cook for another few minutes, or until the broth is absorbed.

FLEXITARIAN TIP: Add Italian sausage to the onion and cook together. Drain before adding the chard.

PER SERVING: CALORIES: 393; TOTAL FAT: 15G; TOTAL CARBS: 61G; FIBER: 11G; SUGAR: 8G; PROTEIN: 8G; SODIUM: 1118MG

CILANTRO-LIME CAULIFLOWER RICE

Prep time: 15 minutes • **Cook time:** 15 minutes

This low-carb version of "rice" can be used as a side dish or added to a Buddha bowl of greens and roasted vegetables. If you want a more tropical approach, use coconut oil in place of the olive oil, and toss with diced mango just before serving. It's a wonderfully versatile dish that goes with just about anything. **SERVES 6**

Dairy-free • **Gluten-free** • **Nut-free** • **Vegan**

1 small head cauliflower or 1 (16-ounce) bag cauliflower rice

2 medium carrots

2 tablespoons olive oil

1 cup thinly sliced scallions

½ tablespoon garlic paste or minced garlic

2 tablespoons freshly squeezed lime juice

Zest of 1 lime

½ cup fresh cilantro, coarsely chopped

1 teaspoon kosher salt

¼ to ½ teaspoon red pepper flakes

1. Grate the fresh cauliflower, if using, and the carrots using a box grater or a food processor fitted with the grater attachment. You should have about 5 cups of grated cauliflower and carrots when you're done.

2. Heat the olive oil in a large skillet over medium-high heat. Add the scallions and garlic. Sauté until softened, about 5 minutes.

3. Add the riced cauliflower and carrots. Cook until tender, stirring occasionally, about 10 minutes.

4. Remove the pan from the heat. Stir in the lime juice, zest, cilantro, salt, and red pepper flakes. Serve warm.

PER SERVING: CALORIES: 79; TOTAL FAT: 5G; TOTAL CARBS: 9G; FIBER: 3G; SUGAR: 4G; PROTEIN: 3G; SODIUM: 434MG

How to Make Cauliflower Rice

There's nothing wrong with purchasing bags of riced cauliflower at your market, but if they don't carry this product, or if you have leftover cauliflower in the refrigerator, you can easily do it yourself.

First remove the leaves from a whole cauliflower and slice off the base root stem. Now pick any of these three ways to make your own cauliflower rice.

Food processor

Chop the cauliflower into large chunks, and place in the bowl of a food processor fitted with the grater blade. Pulse until you have pieces the size of cooked rice. Don't be tempted to blitz for longer or you'll end up with a sauce.

Mini-processor

Chop the cauliflower into small chunks and use a mini-processor in the same way as you would the larger food processor. You will likely need to do this in batches.

Box grater

Use the largest holes on a box grater to rice the cauliflower florets and smaller stems. This might take a few minutes longer, and you may choose not to grate the central root stem, but the cleanup is far easier than ricing with a food processor.

STORE THE CAULIFLOWER RICE in the refrigerator for up to five days in a zipped plastic bag with a paper towel inserted to absorb any moisture, or store in the freezer for up to six months.

FRENCH ONION TOASTS

Prep time: 15 minutes • **Cook time:** 55 minutes

This comforting dish is a toast version of French onion soup, with its trademark caramelized onions and Gruyère cheese, but without a lot of broth. The secret to well-caramelized onions is a long, slow cook over medium-low heat, without moving them around the pan very much. The longer they cook, the more intense the caramel flavor. **SERVES 4**

Nut-free

2 tablespoons olive oil

2 pounds yellow onions, thinly sliced lengthwise

2 teaspoons dried thyme

1 teaspoon kosher salt

1 cup Better Than Bouillon No Beef Base, or vegetable broth

1 tablespoon dry sherry

4 slices crusty bread, such as ciabatta

1 cup grated Gruyère cheese

1. Heat the oil in a large skillet over medium-high heat until it shimmers. Add in the onion slices, thyme, and salt. Use tongs to toss and coat the onions with the oil. Evenly spread the onions across the skillet and reduce the heat to medium-low. Cook for 45 minutes, moving the onions only every 10 to 15 minutes in the beginning and then every few minutes over the last 10 minutes. To caramelize, the onions need direct contact with the hot skillet, but left too long, they'll burn. Use a metal spatula during the final 15 minutes to assist in moving and tossing the onions.

2. Add the broth and sherry to the skillet and scrape up any cooked onion bits from the bottom of the pan. Simmer for 10 minutes.

3. Toast the bread, then place each slice in a shallow bowl. Ladle the onions and a little broth over the bread and top with cheese.

COOKING TIP: For a more hands-off option, the onions can be cooked in a slow cooker on low for 6 to 7 hours, although you'll need to stir them around a few times in the final hour of cooking to evenly caramelize, and the caramelization won't be as deep because of the moist slow cooker environment.

SUBSTITUTION TIP: Gruyère is a type of Swiss cheese, and can be swapped out for Emmentaler or Jarlsberg.

PER SERVING: CALORIES: 332; TOTAL FAT: 17G; TOTAL CARBS: 34G; FIBER: 6G; SUGAR: 11G; PROTEIN: 13G; SODIUM: 939MG

CAULIFLOWER SKILLET STEAKS

Prep time: 15 minutes • **Cook time:** 15 minutes

Cauliflower steaks can be pan-sautéed on the stove or oven-roasted. Rub them with spices, top with a sauce or some melty cheese, or layer over a salad. To cut the steaks from the cauliflower head, trim the stem and remove any leaves. Place the cauliflower cut-side down, then slice into steaks. As you move from the middle, the florets will crumble more, but I just add them to the pan. **SERVES 4**

Dairy-free • **Gluten-free** • **Nut-free** • **Vegan**

1 large head cauliflower, sliced into 6 (1-inch-thick) steaks

2 tablespoons olive oil, divided

½ teaspoon smoked paprika

½ teaspoon kosher salt

¼ teaspoon cayenne pepper

Balsamic Roasted Tomatoes (page 168)

1. Rub both sides of the cauliflower steaks lightly with 1 tablespoon of olive oil, and sprinkle on both sides with the paprika, salt, and cayenne.

2. Heat the remaining 1 tablespoon of olive oil in a large sauté pan over medium-high heat. Arrange the cauliflower steaks in the pan, including any extra florets. You may need to cook the steaks in two batches.

3. Cook the cauliflower until slightly crisped, about 3 minutes per side. Reduce the heat to medium and continue to cook for another 8 to 10 minutes, or until the cauliflower is tender when pierced with a sharp knife.

4. Serve the cauliflower steaks topped with the roasted tomatoes.

PER SERVING: CALORIES: 114; TOTAL FAT: 8G; TOTAL CARBS: 11G; FIBER: 5G; SUGAR: 5G; PROTEIN: 4G; SODIUM: 354MG

EASY MISO RAMEN

Prep time: 15 minutes • **Cook time:** 20 minutes

Ramen is all the rage, with its thick, wavy noodles. In Japan, where it is a national dish, each region has its own version, but all agree that the two major components are the noodles and the broth. The noodles can vary in length and shape, but traditional noodles are wheat-based. Many ingredients, ranging from kelp to shiitake mushrooms, are cooked for a long time with pork or chicken to create a rich broth. In this recipe, the soy sauce, miso, mushrooms, and Better Than Bouillon No Beef Base merge together to create a broth in a fraction of the time. Feel free to add toppings of your choice at the end, such as sliced scallions, chopped fresh basil, thinly-sliced cabbage, or a soft-boiled egg. **SERVES 4**

Dairy-free • **Vegan**

3 tablespoons olive oil

½ yellow onion, coarsely chopped

2 cups chopped broccoli

2 tablespoons garlic paste or minced garlic

2 tablespoons ginger paste or finely chopped fresh ginger

2 heads baby bok choy, coarsely chopped

2 tablespoons soy sauce

1 tablespoon yellow miso

1 cup sliced fresh mushrooms

4 cups vegetable broth

1½ teaspoons Better Than Bouillon No Beef Base

2 cups baby spinach

3½ ounces ramen noodles

1. Heat the olive oil in a large, heavy-bottomed pot over medium-high heat. Add the onion, broccoli, garlic, and ginger and sauté for 5 to 6 minutes.

2. Add the bok choy, soy sauce, miso, and mushrooms and sauté for another 5 minutes.

3. Add the vegetable broth, Better Than Bouillon, spinach, and ramen. Cook for 10 minutes, or until the noodles are cooked through and the vegetables are tender.

4. Serve hot, with optional toppings as desired.

COOKING TIP: For a quick way to make soft-boiled eggs to top this recipe with, use an electric pressure cooker. Add 1 cup of water to the pot, insert the trivet, and arrange the eggs on the trivet. Lock the lid into place and cook for 3 minutes at high pressure for a partially cooked yolk. Immediately perform a quick release, and place the eggs in a bowl of ice water to halt further cooking.

PER SERVING: CALORIES: 267; TOTAL FAT: 11G; TOTAL CARBS: 35G; FIBER: 5G; SUGAR: 4G; PROTEIN: 8G; SODIUM: 1960MG

PURÉED CARROT-GINGER SOUP

Prep time: 15 minutes • **Cook time:** 20 minutes

Carrots can be fibrous in soups and sauces. Adding a little sweet potato goes a long way to adding a silky texture to the mix, with little effort on your part. Just peel and coarsely chop, add to the soup, and purée using a powerful blender, immersion blender, or food processor. **SERVES 4**

Dairy-free • Gluten-free • Nut-free • Vegan

1 tablespoon olive oil

1 pound carrots, cut into
¼-inch-thick disks

½ medium yellow
onion, chopped

1 tablespoon ginger paste

1 tablespoon garlic paste or
1½ tablespoons minced garlic

1 teaspoon kosher salt

4 cups vegetable broth or water

1 small sweet potato, peeled
and diced

1 tablespoon freshly squeezed
lime juice

1. Heat the olive oil in a large, heavy-bottomed pot over medium-high heat. Add the carrots, onion, ginger, garlic, and salt. Sauté until the vegetables slightly soften, about 10 minutes.

2. Stir in the broth and sweet potato, and simmer until the carrots and sweet potato are tender, about 10 minutes. Pour the soup into a blender (in batches, if necessary) and purée until smooth.

3. Return the soup back to the pot and stir in the lime juice.

PER SERVING: CALORIES: 133; TOTAL FAT: 4G; TOTAL CARBS: 25G; FIBER: 5G; SUGAR: 9G; PROTEIN: 2G; SODIUM: 677MG

SPICY CAULIFLOWER SOUP WITH TURMERIC AND YOGURT

Prep time: 20 minutes • **Cook time:** 30 minutes

I keep a stash of store-bought pastes on hand so dishes like this can come together in a snap. The pastes come in handy tubes that keep for weeks in the refrigerator, and they are full of fresh flavor. When I'm at the end of a tube, I cut it in half with scissors and scrape out the last bit, leaving nothing to waste. Look for them in the fresh herb area of the produce section of most markets. **SERVES 4**

Gluten-free • **Nut-free**
Dairy-free and Vegan: Use coconut milk yogurt instead of Greek yogurt

2 tablespoons olive oil

3 large shallots, chopped, or ½ yellow onion

1 tablespoon garlic paste or minced garlic

1 tablespoon ginger paste

2 teaspoons red chili paste

1 teaspoon kosher salt

½ teaspoon ground turmeric

1 (2-pound) cauliflower, coarsely chopped

4 cups vegetable broth or water

½ cup plain Greek yogurt

1. Heat the olive oil in a large, heavy-bottomed pot over medium-high heat. Add the shallots and cook until soft, about 5 minutes. Stir in the garlic paste, ginger paste, red chili paste, salt, and turmeric, and sauté for 3 to 4 minutes to build flavor.

2. Add the cauliflower and broth, and bring to a simmer. Simmer until the cauliflower is tender, 15 to 20 minutes.

3. Using an immersion blender, blend the soup to your preferred consistency. Alternatively, transfer the soup, in batches if necessary, to a blender and purée to your preferred consistency.

4. Stir in the yogurt and adjust any of the seasonings as desired.

PER SERVING: CALORIES: 178; TOTAL FAT: 9G; TOTAL CARBS: 20G; FIBER: 6G; SUGAR: 10G; PROTEIN: 7G; SODIUM: 762MG

CAULIFLOWER, LEEK, AND WHITE BEAN STEW

Prep time: 15 minutes • **Cook time:** 30 minutes

Any white bean will work in this stew, but I always gravitate toward cannellini beans. They have the same ancestor as great northern and navy (pea) beans and taste nearly identical. But the texture of the cannellini is creamier, making it a great choice for soups. If you can't find them, great northern is your next best bet for soups and stews. **SERVES 4**

Dairy-free • **Gluten-free** • **Nut-free** • **Vegan**

1 tablespoon olive oil

1 cup thinly sliced leek, white and light green parts only, or yellow onion

1 tablespoon garlic paste or minced garlic

½ jalapeño pepper, minced

1 teaspoon kosher salt

Pinch freshly ground black pepper

2 cups chopped cauliflower

4 cups vegetable broth

2 cups canned cannellini beans

1. Heat the olive oil in a large, heavy-bottomed pot over medium-high heat. Add the leek, garlic paste, jalapeño, salt, and black pepper, and cook until the vegetables soften and are very fragrant, about 10 minutes.

2. Mix in the cauliflower, then add the vegetable broth and beans. Bring to a simmer and cook until the cauliflower is tender, 15 to 20 minutes.

PER SERVING: CALORIES: 132; TOTAL FAT: 4G; TOTAL CARBS: 20G; FIBER: 6G; SUGAR: 6G; PROTEIN: 6G; SODIUM: 758MG

SMOKY TOMATO SOUP

Prep time: 15 minutes • **Cook time:** 30 minutes

Navy beans, also called pea beans, are small, oval-shaped white beans that become creamy when cooked. Mash some up to thicken a soup or stew, or purée them for a dip. They're mild in flavor and tend to take on the flavors of whatever they're cooked with, making them a perfect partner for flavors that you want to shine. In this soup, they won't get in the way of the tomato and smoky flavors, but they contribute a silky creaminess without any cream. If you don't want any smoke to your soup, just eliminate the chipotles in adobo sauce. **SERVES 4**

Dairy-free • **Gluten-free** • **Nut-free** • **Vegan**

2 tablespoons olive oil, divided

1 cup chopped yellow onion

1 tablespoon garlic paste or minced garlic

1 tablespoon tomato paste

1½ teaspoons dried oregano

1½ teaspoons chipotle chiles in adobo sauce

1½ teaspoons kosher salt, plus more for seasoning

1 (14.5-ounce) can navy (pea) white beans, drained and rinsed

1 cup vegetable broth

2 (28-ounce) cans crushed tomatoes

Freshly ground black pepper

1. Heat the olive oil in a large, heavy-bottomed pot over medium-high heat. Add the onion and sauté until softened, about 10 minutes. Add the garlic and cook for 1 minute, then stir in the tomato paste, oregano, chipotles, and salt. Cook for 2 to 3 minutes, stirring often, until the mixture is very fragrant.

2. Add the beans and sauté for 5 minutes. You may see a little browning on the bottom of the pot.

3. Stir in the vegetable broth, scraping up the brown bits on the bottom. Pour in the tomatoes. Bring to a simmer and cook for 5 minutes.

4. Use an immersion blender to purée the soup. Alternatively, transfer the soup to a blender (in batches, if necessary) and purée until completely smooth. Taste and season with salt and pepper, if needed.

PER SERVING: CALORIES: 316; TOTAL FAT: 8G; TOTAL CARBS: 47G; FIBER: 15G; SUGAR: 11G; PROTEIN: 15G; SODIUM: 1569MG

CRISPY BLACK BEAN BURGERS

Prep time: 45 minutes • **Cook time:** 10 minutes

You may be tempted to skip the oats in this recipe, but in addition to absorbing some of the egg and helping to hold the burger together, the oats make a crispy skin on the burger and create a grittier texture. Without them, your burger will be much softer. If you don't have a food processor, use a blender to chop the oats. Then mash half of the beans with a fork and mix everything together in a large bowl. Just be sure to have wet hands when forming the patties. They're sticky, but won't stick to wet hands. **MAKES 4**

Nut-free
Gluten-free: Use gluten-free buns

½ cup rolled oats

1 (15-ounce) can black beans, drained and rinsed, divided

1 large egg

1 teaspoon ground cumin

½ teaspoon smoked paprika

1 teaspoon kosher salt

¼ teaspoon freshly ground black pepper

½ cup grated pepper jack cheese

2 large scallions, chopped

2 tablespoons tomato-based pasta sauce or basil pesto

2 tablespoons olive oil, divided

4 hamburger buns

Sliced tomato, for topping

Sliced avocado, for topping

1. Place the oats in a blender or food processor and pulse 5 times to roughly chop them. Add half of the beans, the egg, cumin, paprika, salt, and pepper. Blend for about 30 seconds, or until well mixed. Transfer the mixture to a large bowl.

2. Add the remaining beans, the cheese, scallions, and pasta sauce to the bowl and mix until well combined.

3. Lightly oil a plate. With wet hands, divide the bean mixture into four equal amounts and shape into four patties. Place the patties on the plate. Refrigerate for 30 minutes to let the burgers set up.

4. Warm the remaining olive oil in a medium skillet (preferably cast iron) over medium-high heat. Add the burgers and cook, without moving them, until browned with a good crust, 3 to 4 minutes. Carefully flip and continue to cook until the burgers feel firm when pressed with a fingertip, 3 to 5 minutes more.

5. Serve each burger on a bun, topped with tomato and avocado slices.

PER SERVING: CALORIES: 421; TOTAL FAT: 18G; TOTAL CARBS: 49G; FIBER: 11G; SUGAR: 4G; PROTEIN: 18G; SODIUM: 932MG

BUTTERMILK CORNBREAD–TOPPED CHILI

Prep time: 20 minutes • **Cook time:** 50 minutes

We love cornbread at our house, and I often cover casseroles with it since it's so easy to make and saves me a baking pan. In fact, the first time I made this, Carnivorous Maximus blurted out that I was turning him into a vegetarian. There's no higher compliment for a vegetarian meal at our house. You'll need a 14-inch ovenproof skillet, or one large enough to accommodate both the chili and cornbread, without spilling over in the oven. You can also use a medium Dutch oven with great success, as shown on page 102. If you prefer less cornbread, cut the recipe in half, and dollop spoonfuls of the batter onto the chili, cobbler-style. Or you can eliminate the cornbread altogether. **SERVES 6**

Nut-free

FOR THE CHILI

2 tablespoons olive oil

½ onion, diced (about 1 cup)

2 orange bell peppers, diced (about 2 cups)

½ jalapeño pepper, seeded and finely diced

1 tablespoon garlic paste or 1½ tablespoons minced garlic

2 (15-ounce) cans kidney beans, drained and rinsed

1 (28-ounce) can crushed tomatoes

1 tablespoon chili powder

1 teaspoon dried oregano

1 teaspoon kosher salt

½ teaspoon freshly ground black pepper

1. Preheat the oven to 375°F.

2. Heat the oil in the skillet over medium-high heat and add the onion, bell peppers, jalapeño, and garlic. Sauté until the vegetables begin to soften, about 10 minutes. Add the beans, tomatoes, chili powder, oregano, salt, and pepper. Simmer for 10 minutes, or until slightly thickened.

3. In a medium bowl, make the cornbread batter by whisking the cornmeal, flour, sugar, baking soda, and salt together. Form a well in the middle of the dry ingredients. Pour in the eggs, buttermilk, and butter. Whisk together to create a thick batter.

4. Spread the cornbread batter over the top of the chili. Place the skillet on a baking sheet and slide it into the oven. Bake for 30 minutes, or until a knife inserted into the cornbread comes out clean.

FOR THE CORNBREAD

1 cup fine-ground cornmeal

1 cup all-purpose flour

½ cup sugar

½ teaspoon baking soda

¾ teaspoon kosher salt

2 large eggs

1 cup buttermilk

½ cup unsalted butter, melted

SUBSTITUTION TIP: Buttermilk makes the cornbread tender, but if you don't have any on hand, either squeeze 1 tablespoon of lemon juice into 1 cup of milk and let it sit for several minutes or thin some sour cream or yogurt with milk until you have the consistency of buttermilk.

FLEXITARIAN TIP: Add ½ pound cooked and drained ground turkey or ground beef to the chili in place of one of the cans of beans.

PER SERVING: CALORIES: 547; TOTAL FAT: 23G; TOTAL CARBS: 72G; FIBER: 13G; SUGAR: 27G; PROTEIN: 17G; SODIUM: 1230MG

CUBAN SWEET POTATO AND BLACK BEAN TACOS

Prep time: 15 minutes • **Cook time:** 20 minutes

One of the big advantages of tacos is their portability. Because you don't need utensils to eat them, they're a great option to pack up for lunch on a car trip, wrap in foil or paper to take on a hike, or eat on the run as you're walking out the door. The filling can be made ahead and refrigerated for several days, allowing you to throw these together at the last minute. **SERVES 4**

Nut-free
Dairy-free and Vegan: Omit the queso fresco and/or feta cheese toppings

2 tablespoons olive oil

2 medium sweet potatoes, peeled and diced

½ white onion, finely diced

1 teaspoon ground cumin

½ teaspoon kosher salt

1 (15-ounce) can black beans, drained and rinsed

½ cup vegetable broth

8 (8-inch) flour tortillas

½ cup salsa verde

OPTIONAL TOPPINGS

Crumbled queso fresco

Crumbled feta cheese

Shredded cabbage

Thinly sliced radishes

1. Warm the olive oil in a medium sauté pan over medium-high heat. Add the sweet potatoes, onion, cumin, and salt. Sauté until the sweet potatoes begin to soften, about 10 minutes.

2. Add the beans and broth and stir to combine. Bring to a simmer and cook until the sweet potatoes are tender and the beans are warm, about 10 minutes.

3. Lay the tortillas on a flat surface and layer the sweet potato–bean mixture in the middle of the tortillas. Top each with salsa verde. If you choose, you can also garnish each with your preferred taco toppings, such as crumbled queso fresco or feta cheese, shredded cabbage, and thinly sliced radishes.

4. Fold the bottom of each tortilla up and tuck in the sides over the filling. Roll up and wrap in foil, or slice in half and keep together with toothpicks.

FLEXITARIAN TIP: Strips of roasted chicken or grilled flank steak are great additions for the meat eaters, as is chorizo.

PER SERVING: CALORIES: 519; TOTAL FAT: 14G; TOTAL CARBS: 83G; FIBER: 12G; SUGAR: 6G; PROTEIN: 17G; SODIUM: 1195MG

CHICKPEA BOLOGNESE

Prep time: 15 minutes • **Cook time:** 30 minutes

I had my first Bolognese in Italy many years ago, in some long-forgotten neighborhood restaurant. The owner's wife explained it as their daily fresh sauce, or that's what I understood her to say. But it was so much more than that. The meaty sauce shouted its flavor from across the room and was incredibly tender. The secret ingredient, it turns out, was milk. This is my chickpea version of that long-ago food memory. **SERVES 4 TO 6**

Gluten-free • Nut-free

3 tablespoons olive oil

1 (15-ounce) can chickpeas, drained and rinsed

1 cup finely chopped yellow onion

½ cup chopped mushrooms

½ cup finely chopped carrot

1 tablespoon dried oregano

¼ teaspoon kosher salt

¼ teaspoon freshly ground black pepper

½ cup milk

½ cup dry white wine, such as Chardonnay

2½ cups canned chopped tomatoes with their juices

1½ teaspoons balsamic vinegar

1. Heat the olive oil in a large skillet over medium heat. Add the chickpeas, onion, mushrooms, carrot, oregano, salt, and pepper, and stir to combine. Sauté for 5 minutes, or until the chickpeas are very fragrant and the pan is dry. Lightly mash the chickpeas using a fork.

2. Add the milk and simmer until the liquid is completely absorbed, 3 to 4 minutes.

3. Add the white wine and sauté until the liquid is again completely absorbed, 4 to 5 minutes.

4. Stir in the tomatoes and balsamic vinegar, bring to a simmer, and cook for 15 minutes.

SERVING TIP: This Bolognese can be served in the traditional way over pasta, but it's also great over polenta or spaghetti squash noodles.

PER SERVING: CALORIES: 308; TOTAL FAT: 14G; TOTAL CARBS: 34G; FIBER: 9G; SUGAR: 11G; PROTEIN: 10G; SODIUM: 186MG

FARMERS' MARKET
SUMMER ZUCCHINI PASTA

Prep time: 20 minutes • **Cook time:** 10 minutes

Zucchini contains a lot of water, making it a great raw vegetable choice. But all that moisture works against you when sautéeing. If it's sautéed for more than a few minutes, it releases a lot of water into the pan, which waters down the flavor and makes the zucchini soggy. In this recipe, as soon as the zucchini noodles begin to relax into the pan, it's time to remove them and finish up the dish. **SERVES 4**

Gluten-free • Nut-free

1 tablespoon olive oil

¼ serrano chile, seeded and minced

1 tablespoon garlic paste or 6 garlic cloves, minced

1 cup fresh or frozen corn kernels

½ teaspoon kosher salt

3 cups zucchini noodles

10 cherry tomatoes, halved

¼ cup grated Asiago or Parmesan cheese

¼ teaspoon freshly ground black pepper

2 tablespoons Roasted Pumpkin Seeds or Pine Nuts (page 170; optional)

1. Heat the olive oil in a large sauté pan over medium heat. Add the chile and sauté until it softens, about 5 minutes.

2. Add the garlic, corn, and salt. Sauté for about 1 minute. Add the zucchini noodles and sauté for no longer than 3 minutes.

3. Remove the pan from the heat. Add the tomatoes and cheese and toss everything together. Sprinkle with the black pepper and roasted seeds or nuts (if using).

PER SERVING: CALORIES: 135; TOTAL FAT: 9G; TOTAL CARBS: 12G; FIBER: 3G; SUGAR: 6G; PROTEIN: 6G; SODIUM: 376MG

ROASTED RED PEPPER PASTA

Prep time: 10 minutes • **Cook time:** 25 minutes

Feel free to use most any pasta shape in this dish, but I recommend shapes with nooks and crannies that create tiny pockets in which the sauce can pool. Fusilli is a type of pasta that's formed into corkscrew shapes, and it is ideal for holding this sauce. Orecchiette and farfalle are other good options. **SERVES 3**

Nut-free

½ pound fusilli pasta

3 tablespoons olive oil, divided

½ yellow onion, thinly sliced

1 (16-ounce) jar roasted red peppers, drained

2 teaspoons garlic paste or minced garlic

⅓ cup Parmesan cheese, plus more for serving

¼ teaspoon kosher salt

¼ teaspoon freshly ground black pepper

¼ teaspoon red pepper flakes

1. Bring a large pot of salted water to a boil and cook the pasta according to the package directions. Drain and set aside.

2. In the same pot, heat 1 tablespoon of olive oil over medium heat. Add the onion and cook until softened, about 10 minutes. Add the pasta back to the pot and toss to coat with the onion.

3. Blend the roasted red peppers, garlic, cheese, salt, and pepper in a blender or food processor until puréed. Add the remaining 2 tablespoons of olive oil and pulse a few times so that the mixture comes together.

4. Stir the sauce and red pepper flakes into the pasta and cook until the sauce is heated through.

5. Serve with additional Parmesan cheese, if desired.

PER SERVING: CALORIES: 352; TOTAL FAT: 19G; TOTAL CARBS: 38G; FIBER: 2G; SUGAR: 9G; PROTEIN: 11G; SODIUM: 696MG

POTATO GRATIN (PAGE 138)

6

SHEET PAN & BAKING DISH

KOFTA-STYLE CHICKPEA "MEATBALL" PITAS

Prep time: 10 minutes • **Cook time:** 35 minutes

Kofta is street food at its best, and is typically seen in Middle Eastern, Mediterranean, and Asian countries as meatballs on skewers. Each country has its own version, but it's always made with minced or ground meat—often lamb or beef—and is served on flatbreads with yogurt or other sauce. This vegetarian combination of chickpeas and mushrooms results in a meaty flavor that balances perfectly with the aromatic spices. And the fresh, tart tzatziki yogurt sauce is its perfect complement. **SERVES 4**

Nut-free

1 tablespoon unsalted butter

½ cup finely chopped mushrooms

1 (15-ounce) can chickpeas, drained and rinsed

2 teaspoons garlic paste or minced garlic

1 tablespoon dried oregano

1 teaspoon ground allspice

½ teaspoon kosher salt

¼ teaspoon freshly ground black pepper

½ cup panko

1 large egg

2 pita rounds

3 tablespoons Tzatziki (page 175), plus more for serving

Cherry tomatoes, quartered, for serving

Red onion slices

Baby spinach for serving

1. Preheat the oven to 350°F. Line a baking sheet with parchment paper.

2. Melt the butter in a large skillet over medium heat. Add the mushrooms and sauté until softened, about 5 minutes. Add the chickpeas, garlic, oregano, allspice, salt, and pepper, and sauté for another 5 minutes. Coarsely mash the chickpeas with a fork and place everything in a bowl to cool for 5 minutes.

3. Add the panko and egg, and stir with a metal spoon to mix well.

4. Use an ice cream scooper or large spoon to form 8 balls. Place the balls on the prepared baking sheet. Bake for 20 minutes.

5. Cut the pita rounds in half and carefully open the pockets. Spread the tzatziki in the pockets and place 2 chickpea balls, a few tomatoes, red onion, and spinach leaves inside.

6. Serve with additional tzatziki.

PER SERVING: CALORIES: 285; TOTAL FAT: 11G; TOTAL CARBS: 56G; FIBER: 11G; SUGAR: 7G; PROTEIN: 16G; SODIUM: 725MG

SPANISH PAELLA

Prep time: 15 minutes • **Bake time:** 40 minutes

The word *piquillo* means "little beak" in Spanish, and gives this small, tangy pepper its name. Piquillo peppers are only grown in the Navarra region of northern Spain. They're hand-picked, roasted over open fires, hand-peeled, and packed in their own juices. If you can find them, they're worth the trouble. If you can't find them, they have little to no heat, so bell peppers are a good substitute. If you want to add a little more heat to this dish, substitute red Fresno chiles instead. **SERVES 6**

Dairy-free • **Gluten-free** • **Nut-free** • **Vegan**

1 cup short-grain rice, such as Arborio

1 teaspoon olive oil

1¾ cups vegetable broth

1 teaspoon kosher salt

1 teaspoon freshly ground black pepper

¾ teaspoon smoked paprika

4 jarred piquillo or 2 roasted red peppers, cut into thin strips

1 (8-ounce) can fire-roasted tomatoes with their juices

1 (15-ounce) can chickpeas, drained and rinsed

1 cup thinly sliced scallions

¼ cup sliced black olives, such as Kalamata

¼ cup pine nuts

¼ cup chopped fresh parsley or cilantro

1. Arrange an oven rack in the center of the oven and preheat the oven to 350°F.

2. In a small bowl, toss the rice in the olive oil and spread in an even layer on a rimmed baking sheet. Toast in the oven for 5 minutes.

3. Meanwhile, in a medium saucepan over medium heat, bring the broth, salt, pepper, and paprika to a simmer.

4. Add the peppers, tomatoes, and chickpeas to the baking sheet with the toasted rice and stir to combine. Pour the broth over the rice and vegetables. Cover the baking sheet tightly with aluminum foil. Bake for 20 minutes.

5. Uncover the baking sheet and stir the rice. Scatter the scallions, olives, and pine nuts over the rice. Bake, uncovered, for another 15 minutes, or until the rice is tender, with a slightly crispy skin.

6. Transfer the mixture to a serving dish and toss with the parsley.

FLEXITARIAN TIP: Cut a ½-pound cooked Linguiça Portuguese sausage link into ½-inch slices and add them in step 5. Gently press the slices down so that the rice separates around them, allowing the rice to crisp.

PER SERVING: CALORIES: 300; TOTAL FAT: 8G; TOTAL CARBS: 47G; FIBER: 7G; SUGAR: 5G; PROTEIN: 11G; SODIUM: 916MG

VEGGIE AND CHICKPEA FAJITAS

Prep time: 15 minutes • **Cook time:** 30 minutes

When all the kids arrive for a long visit, I try to make meals that allow everyone to build their own plates. With multiple generations in the house, with their numerous preferences, this ensures a happy table. Fajitas are an ideal solution, and are always on the menu for the first night. Best of all, this is a dinner that younger hands can help with. One of my granddaughters is in charge of seasoning everything, and a grandson lays out a buffet of topping options in special bowls. Our favorite toppings include sliced avocado, shredded cheese, sour cream, salsa, and lime wedges. **SERVES 6**

Dairy-free • **Nut-free**
Gluten-free: Use corn tortillas or skip the tortillas entirely

2 bell peppers, any color, sliced into ¼-inch strips

1 large red onion, sliced into ½-inch wedges

2 zucchini, sliced into ½-inch wedges

4 ears corn, kernels sliced off the cob (about 4 cups)

1 (15-ounce) can chickpeas, drained and rinsed

2 tablespoons olive oil

1 tablespoon freshly squeezed lime juice

2 teaspoons ground cumin

2 teaspoons kosher salt, divided

1 teaspoon garlic powder

1 teaspoon freshly ground black pepper, divided

8 (8-inch) flour tortillas

1. Preheat the oven to 450°F. Place one oven rack in the upper third of the oven and another in the lower third. Line two baking sheets with parchment paper.

2. Place the peppers, onion, zucchini, corn kernels, and chickpeas in a large bowl. Add the olive oil, lime juice, cumin, 1 teaspoon of salt, the garlic powder, and ½ teaspoon of pepper, and toss to thoroughly coat the vegetables.

3. Spread the vegetables in an even layer on the baking sheets. Be careful not to crowd the vegetables too close together, as this promotes steaming instead of roasting. Roast for 20 minutes. Stir the vegetables around a little, sprinkle with the remaining salt and pepper, and roast for another 10 minutes, or until the vegetables are tender and just a little charred on the edges.

4. Wrap the tortillas in aluminum foil. Place on one of the baking sheets for the final 5 minutes of roasting.

5. Divide the filling between the tortillas and serve. Finish as desired with your favorite toppings.

PER SERVING: CALORIES: 440; TOTAL FAT: 12G; TOTAL CARBS: 74G; FIBER: 11G; SUGAR: 11G; PROTEIN: 15G; SODIUM: 1337MG

CARAMELIZED FALL VEGETABLES WITH SPICY CHICKPEAS

Prep time: 25 minutes • **Cook time:** 40 minutes

This is a great dish to make for a casual dinner party that celebrates all the flavors of autumn. If you have Crispy Spicy Chickpeas (page 169) on hand, you can use them in place of the spiced chickpea mix in the recipe. Just add them to the sheet pan with the squash and Brussels sprouts for the final 10 minutes of baking to warm them up. But whatever you do, don't skip them entirely. One of our recent dinner guests said their spices mixed with the maple-roasted squash made them a perfect substitute for bacon. **SERVES 6**

Dairy-free • **Gluten-free** • **Nut-free** • **Vegan**

3 tablespoons olive oil, divided

3 tablespoons maple syrup

1 small butternut squash, peeled and cut into 1-inch cubes, or 3 cups precut cubes

2 cups halved Brussels sprouts

1 apple, such as Honeycrisp or Fuji, cored and sliced into 6 wedges

2¼ teaspoons kosher salt, divided

1¼ teaspoons freshly ground black pepper, divided

1 (15-ounce) can chickpeas, drained, rinsed, and dried

¾ teaspoon smoked paprika

½ head green cabbage, sliced into 8 wedges

1 tablespoon garlic paste or finely chopped and mashed garlic

1. Preheat the oven to 400°F. Place an oven rack in the upper and lower thirds of the oven.

2. Mix together 1 tablespoon of olive oil and the maple syrup in a large bowl. Add the squash, Brussels sprouts, and apple slices and toss to coat. Arrange in a single layer on a baking sheet, leaving room for the chickpeas. Sprinkle with 1 teaspoon of salt and ½ teaspoon of black pepper.

3. Make sure the chickpeas are completely dry. Toss them with 1 tablespoon of olive oil, the paprika, ¾ teaspoon of salt, and ¼ teaspoon of pepper. Arrange in a single layer on the same baking sheet with the vegetables.

4. Arrange the cabbage wedges on a second baking sheet. Rub with the remaining 1 tablespoon of olive oil and the garlic. Sprinkle with the remaining ½ teaspoon of salt and ½ teaspoon of pepper.

5. Roast everything for 30 to 40 minutes, or until the vegetables are tender and the cabbage is lightly crisped on the outer edges.

6. Arrange the vegetables and chickpeas on a serving platter or in a bowl, and serve warm.

PER SERVING: CALORIES: 257; TOTAL FAT: 9G; TOTAL CARBS: 42G; FIBER: 9G; SUGAR: 17G; PROTEIN: 8G; SODIUM: 898MG

ACORN SQUASH, SWEET POTATOES, AND APPLES

Prep time: 20 minutes • **Cook time:** 20 minutes

Acorn squash isn't as popular as its butternut cousin, but it shouldn't be shunned. When sliced thinly, the skin is perfectly edible. It's quick and easy to prep (no peeling!), and holds its shape beautifully when roasted. When halved and seeded, it's the perfect-size bowl to hold a hearty salad. Butternut is sweeter and creamier, making it the ideal choice for soups. **SERVES 4**

Gluten-free • Nut-free

1 acorn squash, halved, seeded, and cut into ½-inch wedges

2 sweet potatoes, sliced crosswise into 1-inch disks

2 apples, such as Honeycrisp or Fuji, cored and quartered

1 red onion, cut into 6 wedges

¼ cup Miso Butter (page 174)

2 tablespoons maple syrup

1½ teaspoons kosher salt, divided

1 cup water

1 cup freshly squeezed orange juice

1 cup quinoa

Roasted Pumpkin Seeds (page 170) or store-bought, for serving

1. Preheat the oven to 425°F.

2. Place the squash, sweet potatoes, apples, and onion on a rimmed baking sheet.

3. In a small bowl, whisk together the miso butter, maple syrup, and 1 teaspoon of salt. Drizzle this over the vegetables and apple slices, and toss with your hands to completely coat.

4. Arrange the vegetables and apple slices in a single layer, with as much space between each other as possible. Roast until everything is tender and slightly caramelized, 15 to 18 minutes.

5. Meanwhile, in a saucepan on the stove top, bring the water and orange juice to a boil with the remaining ½ teaspoon salt. Add the quinoa. Reduce the heat to low, cover, and cook at a low simmer until the quinoa is tender, about 15 minutes. Remove the pan from the heat, and keep it covered for 5 minutes. The quinoa will be very tender, and you will see a little curlicue in each seed when it is done.

6. Spread the cooked quinoa on a serving plate, and spoon the roasted vegetables and apple slices over it. Top with roasted pumpkin seeds.

FLEXITARIAN TIP: Add 1 pound bone-in split chicken breasts to the baking sheet, and arrange so that the breasts are directly on the pan, not on the squash or potatoes. Lightly oil the chicken and sprinkle with salt and pepper. Bake everything in a preheated 350°F oven for 40 minutes, or until the internal temperature of the chicken reaches 165°F. Serve everything over the quinoa, and top with the pumpkin seeds.

PER SERVING: CALORIES: 447; TOTAL FAT: 9G; TOTAL CARBS: 85G; FIBER: 12G; SUGAR: 27G; PROTEIN: 10G; SODIUM: 1261MG

STUFFED ROASTED SWEET POTATOES

Prep time: 20 minutes • **Cook time:** 30 minutes

The contrast of the warm spices with the cooling tzatziki makes this a very satisfying and flavorful dish. If you already have Crispy Spicy Chickpeas (page 169) on hand, use those and skip step 3 of the recipe. Add them in the final 10 minutes of roasting to warm them up if you want, although it's not necessary. If you make them with this recipe, as written, you may choose to toss the chickpeas with the spices before roasting to make it easier, but there's some risk the spices may burn and become bitter. **SERVES 4**

Gluten-free • Nut-free

4 medium sweet potatoes, halved lengthwise

1 red onion, quartered

1½ tablespoons olive oil, divided

½ teaspoon kosher salt, divided

¼ teaspoon freshly ground black pepper

1 (15-ounce) can chickpeas, drained, rinsed, and dried

½ teaspoon smoked paprika

½ teaspoon ground cinnamon

¼ teaspoon ground cumin

2 cups baby spinach

1 avocado, peeled and diced

½ cup halved cherry tomatoes

½ cup Tzatziki (page 175)

1. Preheat the oven to 400°F. Lightly oil a baking sheet.

2. Rub the sweet potatoes and onion in 1 tablespoon of olive oil and season with ¼ teaspoon of salt and the pepper. Arrange in a single layer on the baking sheet, with the potatoes cut-side down.

3. In a medium bowl, toss the chickpeas in the remaining ½ tablespoon of olive oil and ¼ teaspoon of salt. Place them on the same baking sheet with the sweet potatoes and onion.

4. Roast for 20 minutes, then flip the potatoes cut-side up and shift the onion and chickpeas around a bit. Roast for another 10 minutes, or until the sweet potatoes are tender when pierced with a fork.

5. Break up the sweet potato flesh with a fork and place it in a medium bowl, and arrange the potato skins on a serving plate. Lightly mash the sweet potato filling with a fork, and add the roasted onion and chickpeas, the paprika, cinnamon, and cumin. Toss together and add the spinach, avocado, and tomatoes. Toss again and scoop into the potato skins.

6. Drizzle with the tzatziki. Serve any extra sauce on the side.

PER SERVING: CALORIES: 482; TOTAL FAT: 24G; TOTAL CARBS: 56G; FIBER: 15G; SUGAR: 13G; PROTEIN: 13G; SODIUM: 610MG

ASIAN STIR-FRY WITH TOFU

Prep time: 30 minutes • **Cook time:** 25 minutes

Tofu contains water and is packed in even more water. To get crispy tofu, that water needs to be drained off. I wrap a block of tofu in a towel, and top it with a plate weighted down by a heavy can. Every 10 minutes, I check the towel to see if it's saturated and needs to be changed. I continue this process for at least 30 minutes. **SERVES 4**

Dairy-free • **Vegan**
Gluten-free: Use gluten-free tamari

8 ounces extra-firm tofu, drained, dried, and cut into ½-inch slices

3 cups broccoli florets

2 carrots, cut diagonally into ½-inch-thick slices

1 bell pepper, any color, sliced into long strips

1 cup halved cremini mushrooms

1 cup snow peas

3 scallions

¼ cup tamari or low-sodium soy sauce

3 tablespoons rice wine vinegar

1½ tablespoons packed brown sugar

1 tablespoon ginger paste or grated fresh ginger

1 tablespoon garlic paste or minced garlic

¼ teaspoon red pepper flakes

¼ cup peanuts, lightly crushed

1. Preheat the oven to 400°F. Lightly oil a baking sheet.

2. Arrange the tofu, broccoli, carrots, bell pepper, mushrooms, snow peas, and scallions in a single layer on the baking sheet.

3. In a small bowl, whisk together the tamari, vinegar, brown sugar, ginger, garlic, and red pepper flakes. Drizzle over the tofu and vegetables, and gently toss to coat.

4. Roast for 10 to 12 minutes. Flip over the tofu slices and continue roasting for another 10 minutes. The tofu should be golden brown, and the vegetables tender.

5. Serve topped with the crushed peanuts

PER SERVING: CALORIES: 212; TOTAL FAT: 8G; TOTAL CARBS: 38G; FIBER: 7G; SUGAR: 12G; PROTEIN: 14G; SODIUM: 1211MG

How to Make Crispy Tofu

The most frequent objection I hear when it comes to eating tofu is to the texture. I'm a firm believer that a crispy tofu is a tofu that can be enjoyed by all. Here are three options for making tofu crispy every time, with different flavoring suggestions.

FOR THE FIRST TWO OPTIONS: Drain 1 (8-ounce) block of extra-firm tofu for 15 to 30 minutes by wrapping it in a towel and weighting it down with a plate topped with a 28-ounce can of tomatoes (or something similar). The less water in the tofu, the crispier it will become.

Crispy Pan-Fried Tofu

¼ cup soy sauce
1 tablespoon brown sugar
Olive oil or sesame oil, for sautéing

1. After draining the tofu, cut it into ½-inch-thick slices.

2. In a medium bowl, prepare the marinade. Combine ¼ cup soy sauce with 1 tablespoon brown sugar. Place the tofu slices in the bowl and coat with the marinade. Let the tofu sit for 30 minutes.

3. In a hot skillet slicked with olive oil or sesame oil, sauté the marinated tofu, cooking for 5 minutes per side, or until the surfaces begin to crisp.

Crispy Baked Tofu

1 tablespoon soy sauce
1 tablespoon olive oil or sesame oil
1 tablespoon cornstarch
½ teaspoon kosher salt

1. Preheat the oven to 400°F.

2. After draining the tofu, cut it into 1-inch cubes.

3. In a medium bowl, drizzle the tofu cubes with soy sauce and oil, and thoroughly coat them with a mixture of the cornstarch and kosher salt.

4. Bake in the oven for 25 to 30 minutes.

Crispy Tofu—Combination Method

¼ teaspoon kosher salt
1 to 2 teaspoons of your favorite seasoning mix
Olive oil or sesame oil, for sautéing

1. Drain the tofu and slice into cubes. Season with the salt and your favorite seasoning mix.

2. Sear for 3 minutes per side in a shimmering hot skillet slicked with olive or sesame oil, and finish in a preheated 375°F oven for 15 minutes.

Crispy Tofu from Frozen

1 (8-ounce) block of extra-firm tofu
¼ teaspoon kosher salt
1 to 2 teaspoons of your favorite seasoning mix
Olive oil or sesame oil, for sautéing

1. Press the water from an 8-ounce block of tofu, slice in half, and freeze overnight. (Freezing gives the tofu a spongy texture when it defrosts, which makes it easier to squeeze out additional liquid before cooking, and makes it even better at soaking up marinades.)

2. When ready to cook, remove the tofu from the freezer, defrost, and squeeze out additional liquid. Slice into ½-inch-thick slices. Toss with the salt and your favorite seasoning mix, and sauté in a hot skillet slicked with olive oil or sesame oil for 5 minutes per side, until the surfaces begin to crisp, or bake at 400°F for 25 to 30 minutes.

CHEESY HASH BROWNS EGG BAKE

Prep time: 10 minutes • **Cook time:** 6 minutes • **Bake time:** 45 minutes

Since we moved to the mountains, we get a lot of weekend guests, and I've needed to create a variety of breakfast dishes for everyone to enjoy. This dish can be either fully baked ahead and warmed in a 350°F oven for 15 to 20 minutes, or assembled the night before, refrigerated, and baked off in the morning. If I have a meat-eating crowd, I sauté ½ pound of sausage with the onions and bell peppers, drain the grease, and add the mixture to the potatoes in step 2. **SERVES 6**

Gluten-free • Nut-free

½ tablespoon unsalted butter, at room temperature

1 tablespoon olive oil

1 medium onion, diced

1 medium bell pepper, any color, diced

1½ teaspoons kosher salt, divided

1 cup baby spinach

½ (30-ounce) bag frozen hash brown potatoes

10 large eggs

1 cup milk

¼ cup sour cream

1 tablespoon Dijon mustard

¼ teaspoon freshly ground black pepper

1½ cups shredded sharp Cheddar cheese

1. Preheat the oven to 375°F. Grease a 9-by-13-inch baking dish with the butter.

2. Warm the oil in a medium skillet over medium heat. Add the onion, bell pepper, and ½ teaspoon of salt and sauté, stirring occasionally, until the vegetables are soft, about 5 minutes. Add the spinach and toss until wilted, about 1 minute.

3. Transfer the mixture to the baking dish. Add the hash browns, stir to combine, and spread into an even layer on the bottom of the dish.

4. In a large bowl, whisk together the eggs, milk, sour cream, mustard, remaining 1 teaspoon of salt, and the pepper. Fold in the cheese. Pour the mixture over the vegetables.

5. Bake for 45 minutes, or until the top is lightly browned and a knife inserted in the middle comes out clean. Let cool for 5 minutes before slicing.

PER SERVING: CALORIES: 356; TOTAL FAT: 26G; TOTAL CARBS: 12G; FIBER: 1G; SUGAR: 5G; PROTEIN: 20G; SODIUM: 945MG

BREAKFAST TAQUITOS CASSEROLE

Prep time: 10 minutes • **Cook time:** 30 minutes

Traditional taquitos are small tortillas wrapped around meat and cheese, and then deep-fried. This recipe is a healthier, baked version designed for breakfast. They're stuffed with eggs, hash browns, and avocado, and topped with salsa verde and cheese. These are best made with flour tortillas, as corn tortillas are prone to tearing and falling apart during the rolling process. **SERVES 4**

Nut-free

2 tablespoons unsalted butter, divided

1½ cups frozen hash browns

1 teaspoon kosher salt, divided

½ teaspoon freshly ground black pepper, divided

6 large eggs, beaten

6 (8-inch) flour tortillas

1 avocado, halved and sliced lengthwise into thin wedges

½ cup salsa verde

⅔ cup grated Cheddar cheese

1. Preheat the oven to 400°F.

2. Melt 1 tablespoon of butter in a medium skillet over medium heat. Add the hash browns, season them with ½ teaspoon of salt and ¼ teaspoon of black pepper, and cook according to the package instructions, about 15 minutes.

3. While the hash browns are cooking, melt the remaining 1 tablespoon of butter in another medium skillet over medium heat. Add the eggs, season with the remaining ½ teaspoon of salt and ¼ teaspoon of pepper, and scramble, about 15 minutes.

4. Wrap the tortillas in a paper towel and warm in the microwave for about 20 seconds so they are more pliable.

5. Lay the tortillas on a flat surface and spoon the hash browns mixture and eggs horizontally across each tortilla, slightly below the center. Place the avocado slices over the eggs. Fold the bottom edge of each tortilla up tightly over the filling, rolling from bottom to top. Place the tortillas seam-side down in a 12-by-12-inch baking dish. Drizzle the salsa over the taquitos and sprinkle with the cheese.

6. Bake until the cheese has melted, 12 to 15 minutes.

PER SERVING: CALORIES: 611; TOTAL FAT: 37G; TOTAL CARBS: 50G; FIBER: 6G; SUGAR: 3G; PROTEIN: 22G; SODIUM: 1457MG

POTATO GRATIN

Prep time: 10 minutes • **Cook time:** 35 minutes

The prep time for this recipe depends entirely on whether you use a chef's knife or a handheld mandoline. A slicing job that takes 15 minutes with a chef's knife can be done in a couple of minutes with a mandoline. But that's not the only benefit of a mandoline. It also allows you to slice a vegetable in even thicknesses, which will allow the slices to cook more evenly. If you use the slider guard, which is provided, or a dishtowel to protect your hands, these mandolines are safe. Some offer a julienne feature in addition to slicing, while others offer slicing in at least three thicknesses and can be locked into a position where the blade is protected. **SERVES 6**

Gluten-free • Nut-free

2 tablespoons unsalted butter, plus more for greasing

2 teaspoons garlic paste or minced garlic

1½ cups 2% milk

¼ cup heavy (whipping) cream

¼ cup vegetable broth

1 red bell pepper, diced

¾ teaspoon kosher salt

¼ teaspoon freshly ground black pepper

2 cups shredded Gruyère or Swiss cheese, divided

2 pounds mixed yellow Yukon Gold potatoes and sweet potatoes

¼ cup finely chopped fresh chives

1. Preheat the oven to 375°F and butter a 2-quart baking dish.

2. In a medium pot, combine the butter, garlic, milk, cream, broth, bell pepper, salt, and pepper, and bring to a gentle simmer over medium heat, about 5 minutes. Be careful not to bring it to a boil. Stir in 1 cup of cheese.

3. While the liquid is coming to a simmer, slice the potatoes thinly. I use a handheld mandoline on the thinnest setting, which slices potatoes ⅛ inch thick in about 30 seconds. You can use a chef's knife, too, but it will take longer.

4. Layer the potatoes in the prepared baking dish and pour the hot milk mixture over them. Sprinkle the remaining 1 cup of cheese on top. Bake for 30 minutes. Allow to rest for 10 minutes before serving.

5. Serve with a flourish of chives.

PER SERVING: CALORIES: 374; TOTAL FAT: 20G; TOTAL CARBS: 32G; FIBER: 2G; SUGAR: 5G; PROTEIN: 16G; SODIUM: 452MG

SWISS CHARD AND ORZO GRATIN

Prep time: 10 minutes • **Cook time:** 20 minutes • **Bake time:** 30 minutes

Orzo pasta is perfect for casseroles because it doesn't take over like its pushier penne cousin. It moves around to accommodate any vegetables you add to the mix, allowing the vegetables to sing. This is a very versatile baked dinner that can be adjusted to swap in other vegetables for the chard. It is special enough for a holiday table. Leftovers can even be served for a hearty breakfast with an egg on top. **SERVES 4**

Nut-free

½ tablespoon unsalted butter, at room temperature

¾ cup orzo

1 (15-ounce) can cannellini or other white beans, drained and rinsed

1 tablespoon olive oil

½ cup chopped shallot

½ teaspoon kosher salt

1 teaspoon freshly ground black pepper

1 cup heavy (whipping) cream

1½ cups vegetable broth

2 large bunches Swiss chard, stems removed and leaves coarsely chopped

½ cup coarsely chopped jarred roasted red peppers

¾ cup grated Parmesan cheese

⅓ cup Lemony Breadcrumbs (page 171)

1. Preheat the oven to 400°F. Grease a 12-by-12-inch baking dish with the butter.

2. Bring a medium pot of well-salted water to a boil. Add the orzo and cook for 5 minutes. The pasta won't be done in that time, but it will finish cooking in the oven. Drain the orzo and spread it across the bottom of the baking dish.

3. Evenly spread the beans over the orzo.

4. Heat the olive oil in a medium skillet over medium heat. Add the shallot, salt, and pepper, and sauté until the shallot is completely softened, about 4 minutes.

5. Stir in the cream and broth and bring to a boil. Reduce the heat to low and simmer until the liquid is reduced to 2 cups, about 10 minutes. Add the Swiss chard in batches, tossing to coat. Cook until the chard is wilted, about 3 minutes.

6. Pour the chard and sauce into the baking dish. Top with the roasted red peppers, followed by the cheese. Finish with a flurry of breadcrumbs.

7. Bake for 25 to 30 minutes.

INGREDIENT TIP: Swiss chard is a vitamin and mineral powerhouse, boasting high levels of vitamin K and potassium. Additionally, it's loaded with antioxidants for fighting inflammation and free-radical damage, and for promoting eye health.

PER SERVING: CALORIES: 544; TOTAL FAT: 33G; TOTAL CARBS: 46G; FIBER: 9G; SUGAR: 4G; PROTEIN: 20G; SODIUM: 944MG

BAKED CHEESY BROCCOLI WITH QUINOA

Prep time: 15 minutes • **Cook time:** 45 minutes

This recipe is a perfect example of adding quinoa to increase the protein and nutrition of a dish. Technically a seed, quinoa is cooked and eaten like a grain. But it is significantly more nutritious than a common grain. It boasts a higher fiber content than brown rice and supports improved gut health. Additionally, it's high in antioxidants, is gluten-free, and is considered a complete protein, which means it provides all the essential amino acids our bodies need. **SERVES 8**

Gluten-free • Nut-free

½ tablespoon unsalted butter, at room temperature

1½ cups bite-size broccoli pieces or frozen broccoli florets

2 large eggs

1 cup whole or 2% milk

1 tablespoon Dijon mustard

1 teaspoon kosher salt

½ teaspoon freshly ground black pepper

½ yellow onion, diced

2 teaspoons garlic paste or 5 garlic cloves, minced

2 cups cooked quinoa (see page 55)

1½ cups grated Cheddar cheese

½ cup Lemony Breadcrumbs (page 171)

1. Preheat the oven to 350°F. Grease a 9-by-13-inch baking dish with the butter.

2. Fill a medium pot with about 2 inches of water and add a steamer. Bring to a boil and add the broccoli. Steam until just tender, about 10 minutes.

3. In a large bowl, beat together the eggs, milk, mustard, salt, and pepper. Fold in the broccoli, onion, garlic, quinoa, and cheese. Pour everything into the baking dish. Top with the breadcrumbs.

4. Bake for 35 to 40 minutes.

SUBSTITUTION TIP: Swap cauliflower for the broccoli, and add 1½ teaspoons of curry powder.

PER SERVING: CALORIES: 243; TOTAL FAT: 11G; TOTAL CARBS: 23G; FIBER: 3G; SUGAR: 3G; PROTEIN: 13G; SODIUM: 538MG

MEXICAN CASSEROLE

Prep time: 15 minutes • **Cook time:** 35 minutes

This casserole is a summer crowd-pleaser. It comes together quickly in the kitchen, and disappears almost as quickly at the table. It's well-suited to make ahead and warm up in a 350°F oven for 15 to 20 minutes before serving. If that's your plan, spread the final ½ cup of cheese (in step 4) on the casserole just before you reheat it. **SERVES 6**

Gluten-free • Nut-free

Olive oil, for greasing

1 cup cooked quinoa (page 55)

1 (15-ounce) can black beans, drained and rinsed

1 cup fresh or frozen corn kernels

1 cup halved cherry tomatoes

2 bell peppers, any color, diced

⅓ cup chopped red onion

1½ tablespoons freshly squeezed lime juice

1½ teaspoons ground cumin

2 teaspoons kosher salt

2 cups grated Monterey Jack cheese, divided

2 tablespoons Roasted Pumpkin Seeds (page 170; optional)

1. Preheat the oven to 400°F. Lightly oil a 9-by-11-inch baking dish.

2. Combine the cooked quinoa, black beans, corn, tomatoes, bell peppers, onion, lime juice, cumin, salt, and 1½ cups of cheese in a large bowl.

3. Spread evenly in the baking dish. Bake for 30 minutes.

4. Spread the remaining ½ cup of cheese over the top of the casserole. Bake for another 5 minutes.

5. Sprinkle the pumpkin seeds over the top (if using). Serve warm.

PER SERVING: CALORIES: 325; TOTAL FAT: 14G; TOTAL CARBS: 33G; FIBER: 8G; SUGAR: 4G; PROTEIN: 18G; SODIUM: 1037MG

CURRIED CAULIFLOWER TETRAZZINI

Prep time: 15 minutes • **Cook time:** 55 minutes

Chicken tetrazzini, with its creamy sauce, pasta, and chicken, is a favored comfort food for all generations. When I began eliminating meat from my diet, this was a dish I knew I would miss. So I began by simply replacing chicken with cauliflower, but it didn't have quite enough flavor on its own. Once I added some curry to the dish, however, I liked it even better than the original chicken dish. **SERVES 6**

Nut-free

2½ tablespoons unsalted butter, divided

1 medium cauliflower, cut into bite-size pieces, or 4 cups frozen florets

2 small leeks, white and light greens parts only, diced

2 tablespoons olive oil

2½ teaspoons curry powder, divided

2 teaspoons kosher salt, divided

1 teaspoon freshly ground black pepper, divided

½ pound spaghetti

3 tablespoons all-purpose flour

1 cup milk

½ cup sour cream or plain Greek yogurt

1 tablespoon garlic paste or minced garlic

1 cup grated Parmesan cheese, divided

½ cup Lemony Breadcrumbs (page 171)

1. Preheat the oven to 400°F. Grease a 9-by-13-inch baking dish with ½ tablespoon of butter.

2. Place the cauliflower and leeks in the baking dish and toss with the olive oil, 1½ teaspoons of curry powder, 1 teaspoon of salt, and ½ teaspoon of black pepper. Roast until the cauliflower pieces are tender and begin to brown, about 30 minutes.

3. While the cauliflower is roasting, bring a large pot of salted water to a boil. Break the spaghetti into thirds so that the noodles are all around 3 inches long. Add to the boiling water and cook according to the package instructions. Drain.

4. Melt the remaining 2 tablespoons of butter in a medium skillet over medium heat. Once it's bubbling, whisk in the flour until the butter becomes a paste. Cook, stirring constantly, for 1 minute. Gradually whisk the milk into the paste. Add the sour cream, garlic, ½ cup of Parmesan, the remaining 1 teaspoon of salt, ½ teaspoon of black pepper, and 1 teaspoon of curry powder, and whisk to thoroughly mix.

5. Fold in the cooked spaghetti. Pour this over the roasted vegetables and lightly toss together. Top with the remaining ½ cup of Parmesan and the breadcrumbs.

6. Lower the oven temperature to 350°F and bake for 15 minutes, or until bubbly.

SUBSTITUTION TIP: Swap out the cauliflower for broccoli or butternut squash.

FLEXITARIAN TIP: Since this dish was made famous with chicken, just replace the cauliflower with 4 cups diced cooked chicken. You can eliminate the curry if you wish, but it goes well with chicken, too.

PER SERVING: CALORIES: 425; TOTAL FAT: 18G; TOTAL CARBS: 52G; FIBER: 6G; SUGAR: 7G; PROTEIN: 17G; SODIUM: 1104MG

BAKED EGGPLANT PARMESAN

Prep time: 20 minutes · **Cook time:** 1 hour

Eggplant is a vegetable I made friends with late in life. Tasting it in a soup with roasted tomatoes while I was in culinary school was my first eye-opener, and it convinced me to try other dishes I'd long ignored. This recipe is my favorite example. Many eggplant Parmesan dishes begin with breading and frying the eggplant, but this healthier version is baked instead. For an extra flavor punch, the breading includes a basil pesto. This recipe will make an eggplant lover out of most anyone. **SERVES 8**

Nut-free

---

2 medium eggplants

2 large eggs, beaten

⅓ cup basil pesto

4 cups Italian breadcrumbs

1 cup Parmesan cheese

6 cups Tomato-Mushroom Ragù (page 148) or 2 (24-ounce) jars tomato-based pasta sauce

2 cups shredded mozzarella cheese, divided

1. Preheat the oven to 375°F. Line a baking sheet with parchment paper.

2. Slice the eggplants into ½-inch rounds.

3. In a small bowl, whisk the eggs together with the pesto. In a second small bowl, combine the breadcrumbs and Parmesan cheese.

4. Dip an eggplant slice into egg-pesto mixture. Let the excess drip off, then dip it in the breadcrumbs and coat it on both sides. Place the slice on the baking sheet. Repeat for all the eggplant slices, and arrange them on the baking sheet in a single layer.

5. Bake the eggplant for 20 minutes. Flip the slices over and bake for 20 minutes more.

6. Increase the oven temperature to 400°F. In a 9-by-13-inch baking dish, spread just enough tomato sauce to cover the bottom. Layer half of the eggplant slices in the bottom of the baking dish. Top them with one-third of the mozzarella, followed by half of the remaining sauce. Repeat with the remaining eggplant, the second third of cheese, and the remaining sauce. Sprinkle the remaining cheese over the top.

7. Bake for 20 minutes. Let sit for 5 minutes before serving.

INGREDIENT TIP: If you find eggplant to be too bitter for you, place the slices in a colander and generously salt them. Let them sit for 1 hour. Rinse, pat dry, and begin the recipe with step 3.

PER SERVING: CALORIES: 423; TOTAL FAT: 14G; TOTAL CARBS: 57G; FIBER: 10G; SUGAR: 15G; PROTEIN: 19G; SODIUM: 1015MG

ASPARAGUS AND PEA RISOTTO (PAGE 165)

7

SLOW COOKER & PRESSURE COOKER

TOMATO-MUSHROOM RAGÙ

Prep time: 15 minutes • **Cook time:** 4 to 5 hours on high or 7 to 8 hours on low

A great ragù recipe is like a little black dress: perfect for most occasions. Serve this over mashed chickpeas or pasta, or ladle it over lentil or chickpea "meatballs." It can even be used as the tomato base on a pizza or as a substitute for canned tomatoes in soups and stews. With this made in advance, dinner is assembled in a snap. It can be refrigerated for up to a week in an airtight container, or frozen for up to six months. **SERVES 6**

Dairy-free • **Gluten-free** • **Nut-free** • **Vegan**

1 tablespoon olive oil

1 yellow onion, diced

1 serrano chile, finely diced

1 tablespoon garlic paste or minced garlic

1 teaspoon dried oregano

1 teaspoon kosher salt

1 teaspoon freshly ground black pepper

2 (28-ounce) cans crushed tomatoes

8 ounces white mushrooms, sliced

1 (6-ounce) can tomato paste

1 tablespoon balsamic vinegar

¼ cup halved Kalamata olives

1. **TO SAUTÉ FIRST:** If your slow cooker has an aluminum insert, set it on the stove top over medium heat. If you don't have an aluminum insert, set a skillet on the stove top over medium heat instead. Heat the oil, then add the onion, chile, garlic, oregano, salt, and pepper. Sauté for 5 minutes. Return the insert to the slow cooker, or add the sautéed ingredients from the skillet to the slow cooker. Add all of the remaining ingredients.

   TO SKIP SAUTÉING: Preheat the slow cooker. Add the onions and cover. While the onions sweat, prep the remaining ingredients. After approximately 10 minutes, remove the cover and add all of the remaining ingredients to the slow cooker.

2. Cook on high for 4 to 5 hours or on low for 7 to 8 hours.

MAKE IT FASTER: Add the oil, onion, chile, garlic, oregano, salt, and pepper to the inner cooking pot of an electric pressure cooker. Select the sauté function, and cook for 5 minutes. Add the crushed tomatoes, mushrooms, tomato paste, vinegar, and olives. Cook on high pressure for 10 minutes. Quick release the pressure.

FLEXITARIAN TIP: Sauté 1 pound of ground beef or pork on the stove. Drain, and add to the slow cooker with the other ingredients.

PER SERVING: CALORIES: 156; TOTAL FAT: 1G; TOTAL CARBS: 31G; FIBER: 11G; SUGAR: 20G; PROTEIN: 9G; SODIUM: 976MG

WHITE BEAN AND ARTICHOKE STEW

Prep time: 15 minutes • **Cook time:** 4 to 5 hours on high or 7 to 8 hours on low

You may see at least five types of dried white beans on your grocery shelves. Navy (pea) beans are interchangeable with great northern beans and flageolet beans (tinged a light green in their dried form) but should not be swapped out for dried cannellini or white kidney beans when using the slow cooker. Kidney beans contain a toxin that can make you ill if the beans are not first boiled for at least 10 minutes and drained before adding to the slow cooker. **SERVES 6**

Dairy-free • **Gluten-free** • **Nut-free** • **Vegan**

1 (13- to 15-ounce) jar marinated artichoke hearts

7 cups vegetable broth or water

2 cups dried navy (pea) beans

2 large celery stalks, thinly sliced

1 medium yellow onion, diced

½ medium carrot, diced

½ teaspoon dried rosemary

1 teaspoon kosher salt

½ teaspoon freshly ground black pepper

1. Drain the artichokes and remove any tough outer leaves.

2. Place the artichokes in the slow cooker along with the broth, beans, celery, onion, carrot, rosemary, salt, and pepper.

3. Cover and cook on high for 4 to 5 hours or on low for 7 to 8 hours.

MAKE IT FASTER: Place the ingredients in an electric pressure cooker and cook on high pressure for 45 minutes. Naturally release the pressure. If using canned beans, reduce the broth or water to 4 cups and cook on high pressure for 10 minutes. Quick release the pressure.

FLEXITARIAN TIP: Purchase a roasted chicken at the market, shred the meat into strips, and stir into the stew before serving. Or add 2 skinless, boneless chicken breasts to the slow cooker with the other ingredients. When cooking is complete, remove the chicken and shred it, then stir it back into the soup.

PER SERVING: CALORIES: 329; TOTAL FAT: 6G; TOTAL CARBS: 48G; FIBER: 19G; SUGAR: 5G; PROTEIN: 22G; SODIUM: 1430MG

FOOD TRUCK SPAGHETTI SQUASH TACO BOWL

Prep time: 15 minutes
Cook time: 2½ hours on high or 5 to 6 hours on low, plus 1 more hour on high

Food trucks around the country are creating new veggie taco bowl variations ranging from zucchini with charred corn to roasted root vegetables. In other words, feel free to have some fun with your own combinations. Add cabbage slaw, Mexican crema, avocado, or your favorite corn salsa. If you want a little extra protein, fry up an egg or some tofu and add it on top. After all, it's your lunch (or dinner)! This version swaps in a spaghetti squash for the bowl. **SERVES 2**

Gluten-free • **Nut-free**
Dairy-free and Vegan: Use vegan mozzarella or eliminate the cheese

1 small (2- to 3-pound) spaghetti squash

1 (15-ounce) can black beans, drained and rinsed

¼ cup grated Mexican cheese blend

½ teaspoon chili powder

¼ teaspoon kosher salt

2 slices lime

15 to 20 cherry tomatoes

2 tablespoons chopped fresh cilantro or store-bought cilantro paste

2 tablespoons Roasted Pumpkin Seeds (page 170)

1. Place the spaghetti squash, whole, in your slow cooker.

2. Cover and cook on high for 2½ hours or low for 5 to 6 hours.

3. Place the squash on a cutting board. Slice off the ends and cut in half lengthwise. Scoop out the seeds with a fork or spoon and discard them.

4. Divide the beans, cheese, chili powder, salt, and lime juice between the two squash halves, and toss together. Return the squash halves to the slow cooker, arranging them side by side. (Slicing off the ends should allow the squash to neatly fit in the cooker.)

5. Cover and cook on high for 1 hour.

6. Use a fork to scrape the flesh of the squash under the beans and cheese to pull up the noodle-like strands. Squeeze a little lime juice on top, and lightly toss.

7. Top the squash with tomatoes, cilantro, and pumpkin seeds. Serve immediately.

MAKE IT FASTER: Pour 1 cup of water into the inner cooking pot of an electric pressure cooker. Place the steamer rack on the bottom, and position the spaghetti squash on the rack. Trim the ends of the squash if needed. Lock the lid into place, and cook for 25 minutes on high pressure. Quick release the pressure. Remove the squash and set aside to cool. Discard any water from the inner pot. Select sauté, add the beans with a little olive oil, and cook until the beans are heated through. Slice the squash in half, scoop out and discard the seeds, and scrape up the spaghetti noodles. Add the beans, cheese, chili powder, salt, and lime juice. Toss to melt the cheese. Top with the tomatoes, cilantro, and pumpkin seeds.

PER SERVING: CALORIES: 429; TOTAL FAT: 6G; TOTAL CARBS: 82G; FIBER: 17G; SUGAR: 5G; PROTEIN: 22G; SODIUM: 432MG

BARBECUE LENTIL SLOPPY JOES

Prep time: 10 minutes • **Cook time:** 3 to 4 hours on high or 6 to 7 hours on low

Lentils are one of the most nutritious and versatile plant-based proteins, but they're not all created equally. French lentils (Le Puy) are a type of green lentils that have a slight peppery flavor. They hold their shape beautifully but take the longest to cook on the stove top, about 45 minutes. This recipe features French lentils with a mostly hands-off slow cooker treatment. For total ease, you can skip the sauté step, but I include this option to create maximum flavor. **SERVES 4**

Dairy-free • **Nut-free** • **Vegan**

1 tablespoon olive oil

1 yellow onion, diced

2 red bell peppers, diced

1 tablespoon garlic paste or finely chopped garlic

1 tablespoon chili powder

1½ cups French green lentils

1½ cups vegetable broth or water

1½ teaspoons kosher salt

¼ cup barbecue sauce

2 tablespoons packed brown sugar

1 (28-ounce) can crushed tomatoes

4 large sandwich rolls, split open and lightly toasted, for serving

1. **TO SAUTÉ FIRST:** If your slow cooker has an aluminum insert, set it on the stove top over medium heat. If you don't have an aluminum insert, set a skillet on the stove top instead. Heat the olive oil. Add the onion, peppers, garlic, and chili powder, and sauté for 10 minutes. Return the insert to the slow cooker, or place the ingredients sautéed in the skillet into the slow cooker. Add all of the remaining ingredients, except the sandwich rolls.

   TO SKIP SAUTÉING: Preheat the slow cooker. Place all of the ingredients, except the sandwich rolls, into the slow cooker.

2. Cover and cook on high for 3 to 4 hours or low for 6 to 7 hours.

3. Ladle the cooked lentils over the toasted sandwich rolls.

MAKE IT FASTER: Select the sauté function on your electric pressure cooker. Heat the olive oil in the inner pot, then add the onion, peppers, garlic, and chili powder. Sauté until the vegetables begin to soften, about 3 minutes. Stir in the lentils, broth, salt, barbecue sauce, brown sugar, and tomatoes. Lock the lid into place, and cook on high pressure for 20 minutes. Naturally release the pressure.

PER SERVING: CALORIES: 559; TOTAL FAT: 4G; TOTAL CARBS: 103G; FIBER: 29G; SUGAR: 17G; PROTEIN: 29G; SODIUM: 1,621MG

BUTTERNUT SQUASH AND BARLEY RISOTTO

Prep time: 10 minutes • **Cook time:** 4 hours on low

The scouring process barley undergoes to remove its hull results in a softer grain called pearl barley. Although much of the nutritional germ and bran is stripped away along with the hull, this softer grain releases more starch into its cooking liquid, making it a good thickener for soups and the perfect base for a creamy risotto that retains a balance of chewiness. If you'd rather the risotto cook longer, use hulled barley and cook on low for 6 to 8 hours. The risotto won't be as creamy as with pearl barley, but it'll be just as delicious. **SERVES 6**

Nut-free

1½ cups pearl barley

2 tablespoons olive oil

2 cups butternut squash, peeled and cubed, or 1 (12-ounce) bag frozen diced butternut squash

1 small yellow onion, diced

4 cups vegetable broth

¼ cup dry white wine, such as Chardonnay

2 teaspoons dried rubbed sage

2 teaspoons kosher salt

¼ teaspoon freshly ground black pepper

¼ cup grated Swiss cheese, for finishing

1. Stir together the barley and olive oil in the slow cooker. Add the butternut squash, onion, broth, wine, sage, salt, and pepper to the cooker, and stir to combine.

2. Cook on low for 4 hours, then check the barley. If it's still slightly hard, continue to cook until it reaches your desired tenderness.

3. Stir in the cheese, and serve immediately.

MAKE IT FASTER: Select sauté on an electric pressure cooker, and heat the olive oil. Add the barley, squash, onion, sage, salt, and pepper and sauté for 8 to 10 minutes, or until the barley begins to toast and the squash begins to caramelize on the bottom. Add the wine and cook for 5 minutes more, or until the wine is almost absorbed. Pour in the broth. Lock the lid in place and cook on high pressure for 25 minutes. Quick release the pressure, and stir in the cheese.

PREP TIP: The best way I've found to peel butternut squash is with either a potato peeler or a sharp chef's knife. First, slice the squash in half, so it can safely lie on a flat side while being peeled. If the squash is difficult to slice in half, microwave the squash for 2 minutes.

PER SERVING: CALORIES: 293; TOTAL FAT: 8G; TOTAL CARBS: 47G; FIBER: 9G; SUGAR: 3G; PROTEIN: 10G; SODIUM: 1100MG

EASY LASAGNA

Prep time: 10 minutes • **Cook time:** 3 to 4 hours on high or 6 to 7 hours on low

Lasagnas loaded with vegetables and then cooked in the slow cooker can easily become lasagna soup. Layering the lasagna with dried mushrooms is the secret, as they'll absorb all that lovely liquid. **SERVES 6**

Nut-free

1 (24-ounce) jar tomato-based pasta sauce or 6 cups Tomato-Mushroom Ragù (page 148)

7 dried lasagna noodles, depending on the size of your slow cooker

15 ounces part-skim ricotta cheese

2 cups baby kale or baby spinach

2 red bell peppers, sliced into long strips

1 cup (4 ounces) dried mushrooms

2 cups shredded mozzarella cheese

1. Spread 1 cup of pasta sauce on the bottom of your slow cooker. This ensures the noodles won't stick.

2. Break the noodles to fit, and cover the bottom of the slow cooker as much as possible, given its shape. Overlap them as necessary. Layer half each of the ricotta, kale, bell peppers, and dried mushrooms over the noodles. Layer one-third of the mozzarella over the mushrooms.

3. Place another layer of noodles over the cheese and cover them with 1 cup of pasta sauce. Layer the remaining ricotta, kale, red peppers, and dried mushrooms over the sauce and top it with another third of mozzarella. Arrange the final layer of pasta noodles over everything, and cover with the remaining sauce and mozzarella.

4. Cover and cook on high for 3 to 4 hours or on low for 6 to 7 hours.

5. Slice the lasagna in the pot, and use a spatula to lift out individual servings.

MAKE IT FASTER: Pour 1 cup of water into the inner cooking pot of an electric pressure cooker, then place the steamer rack inside. Grease a round 6- or 7-inch baking pan. Create layers in the baking pan as described in steps 1, 2, and 3. Press down slightly on the layers to compress as needed. Cover the pan with aluminum foil and place on the steamer rack. Lock the lid in place and cook on high pressure for 20 minutes. Naturally release the pressure. Remove the pan, uncover, and place under a preheated broiler for 3 to 4 minutes to crisp the top cheese layer.

PER SERVING: CALORIES: 375; TOTAL FAT: 9G; TOTAL CARBS: 53G; FIBER: 3G; SUGAR: 8G; PROTEIN: 21G; SODIUM: 398MG

BRUSSELS SPROUTS WITH APPLE AND LEMON

Prep time: 15 minutes • **Pressure cook:** 2 minutes • **Sauté:** 6 minutes
Pressure: high • **Release:** quick

The pressure cooker is perfect for vegetables that take a long time to cook, such as beets and artichokes. Not including the time it takes to heat up the cooker (about 10 minutes), Brussels sprouts are ready in just 2 minutes! **SERVES 2**

Dairy-free • Nut-free • Vegan

½ pound Brussels sprouts, trimmed and halved

1 tablespoon olive oil

½ apple, unpeeled, cored, and cut into bite-size chunks

3 thin slices lemon

⅛ teaspoon celery salt

¼ teaspoon dried sage

2 teaspoons apple cider vinegar

2 tablespoons Lemony Breadcrumbs (page 171)

1. Pour 1 cup of water into the inner cooking pot of the pressure cooker, then place the steamer rack inside. Arrange the Brussels sprouts on the rack. Some halves may fall into the water, but that's fine.

2. Lock the lid in place. Cook on high pressure for 2 minutes.

3. When the cooking is complete, quick release the pressure. Unlock and remove the lid. Drain and set the Brussels sprouts aside.

4. Select the sauté function. Add the oil, along with the apple, lemon slices, celery salt, and sage. Sauté for 2 minutes, or until the apple chunks begin to soften. Add the cooked Brussels sprouts and toss to coat. Sauté for another 4 minutes, or until they begin to crisp. Transfer everything to a serving bowl.

5. Add the cider vinegar to the inner pot, scraping up any bits on the bottom. Pour over the Brussels sprouts and apples, and toss. Top with the breadcrumbs.

MAKE IT SLOWER: Swap out the olive out for 1 tablespoon of unsalted butter. Melt the butter in the slow cooker, and add everything except the apple and breadcrumbs. Cover and cook on high for 1 to 2 hours or on low for 3 to 4 hours. Stir in the apple in the last 30 minutes of cooking. Cover and continue cooking. Top with the breadcrumbs before serving.

PER SERVING: CALORIES: 166; TOTAL FAT: 8G; TOTAL CARBS: 23G; FIBER: 6G; SUGAR: 9G; PROTEIN: 5G; SODIUM: 98MG

SPINACH AND LENTIL SOUP

Prep time: 15 minutes • **Sauté:** 5 minutes • **Pressure cook:** 15 minutes
Pressure: high • **Release:** natural

This recipe is based on the first one my mom gave me when I left home. It was a favorite around our house, especially on cold winter nights. When I moved to New England, I often made a big batch over the weekend, and poured it into jars so dinner could be ready for me in minutes after slogging home from work in the snow. After all these years, and hundreds of soups later, it's still one of my favorites. **SERVES 6**

Gluten-free • **Nut-free**

5 tablespoons olive oil, divided

1 small onion, diced

2 carrots, chopped

2 celery stalks, thinly sliced

2 cups green lentils, rinsed

2 medium Yukon Gold
    potatoes, diced

5 cups vegetable broth

1 (8-ounce) can fire-roasted
    tomatoes with their juices

2 teaspoons dried oregano

1½ teaspoons kosher salt

½ teaspoon freshly ground
    black pepper

⅓ cup half-and-half

3 cups packed fresh
    baby spinach

1 tablespoon sherry wine vinegar

1. Select the sauté function on your pressure cooker. When the inner cooking pot is warm, add 2 tablespoons of olive oil. Add the onion, carrots, and celery and sauté for about 5 minutes, until the vegetables are softened and fragrant. Add the lentils, potatoes, broth, tomatoes, oregano, salt, and pepper.

2. Lock the lid in place. Select the soup function, if your pressure cooker has one, or cook on high pressure for 15 minutes.

3. When cooking is complete, naturally release the pressure. Unlock and remove the lid.

4. Stir in the half-and-half and spinach leaves until they are wilted. Taste and season with additional salt and pepper, if needed.

5. Serve in bowls, drizzled with the remaining 3 tablespoons of olive oil and the sherry wine vinegar.

MAKE IT SLOWER: Heat a skillet or your slow cooker's aluminum insert (if it has one) on the stove top over medium heat. Place the olive oil, onion, carrots, and celery in it, and sauté for about 5 minutes. Transfer the sautéed ingredients to the slow cooker, and add the remaining ingredients. Cover and cook on low for 7 to 8 hours. Stir in the half-and-half and spinach. Serve with a drizzle of olive oil and sherry wine vinegar.

FLEXITARIAN TIP: Eliminate 2 tablespoons of extra-virgin olive oil and sauté ⅔ pound of spicy Italian sausage with the onion, carrot, and celery in step 1.

PER SERVING: CALORIES: 456; TOTAL FAT: 20G; TOTAL CARBS: 49G; FIBER: 22G; SUGAR: 5G; PROTEIN: 22G; SODIUM: 1314MG

How to Use Different Kinds of Lentils

Are all lentils the same, whether black, brown, green, red, or yellow? Yes and no. They're all in the pulse family and have similar nutritional benefits, but they take different lengths of time to cook (which is important to know if you substitute lentils in a recipe), and some hold their shape much better than others. Here's a quick primer on the different types of lentils and when to use them.

Red and yellow lentils

Popular in Indian dishes, these lentils take 15 to 20 minutes to cook, and are slightly mushy.

- Great for thickening soups or purées

Black lentils

Also referred to as beluga lentils, these are the healthiest lentils. They take about 25 minutes to cook, and hold their shape beautifully.

- Perfect for adding to salads

Brown lentils

These are what I call "compromise" lentils. They take 30 to 40 minutes to cook, and hold their shape fairly well.

- Can be either mashed or used with salads

Green, French green, and Le Puy lentils

The longest-cooking lentils, taking about 45 minutes, these hold their shape very well. They are considered to have the best overall flavor and texture, and can be the most expensive option.

- Best in salads or mixed with rice, in tomato sauces, or with roasted vegetables

BLACK BEAN SOUP

Prep time: 10 minutes • **Sauté:** 5 minutes • **Pressure cook:** 10 minutes
Pressure: high • **Release:** 2 minutes natural, then quick

This is my go-to pantry meal since I always have these ingredients on hand, but I often switch up the toppings. Sour cream spiked with a little adobo sauce and grated Mexican cheeses make a regular appearance, and I've even topped this chili with a fried egg and a dollop of guacamole. But I always serve it with warm tortillas on the side. **SERVES 4**

Dairy-free • **Gluten-free** • **Nut-free** • **Vegan**

1 tablespoon olive oil

2 bell peppers, any color, diced

1 yellow onion, chopped

2 cups vegetable broth or water

2 (15-ounce) cans black beans with their liquid

1 (15-ounce) can diced fire-roasted tomatoes with their juices

1 tablespoon freshly squeezed lime juice

1 teaspoon chili powder

1 teaspoon kosher salt

1. Select the sauté function on your pressure cooker. In the inner cooking pot, heat the olive oil. Add the peppers and onion and sauté until softened, 3 to 5 minutes.

2. Add the broth, black beans, tomatoes, lime juice, chili powder, and salt.

3. Lock the lid in place. Select the soup function if your pressure cooker has one, or cook on high pressure for 10 minutes.

4. When cooking is complete, naturally release the pressure for 2 minutes, then quick release the remaining pressure.

5. If you like your black bean soup partially puréed, use an immersion blender in the inner pot of the pressure cooker for 5 to 20 seconds, depending upon how smooth you like it.

6. Serve as is, or with the toppings of your choice.

MAKE IT SLOWER: Pile all the ingredients, except the olive oil, into the slow cooker. Cover and cook on low for 6 to 8 hours. Or swap the cooked beans for 1 cup of dried beans, add 2 additional cups of water or broth, and cook on low for 10 hours. To intensify the flavor, sauté the vegetables on the stove before adding them to the slow cooker.

FLEXITARIAN TIP: Add 4 ounces Spanish chorizo, a type of chorizo that is dried and cured and doesn't require precooking, in step 1 and sauté for some extra flavor.

PER SERVING: CALORIES: 210; TOTAL FAT: 5G; TOTAL CARBS: 31G; FIBER: 10G; SUGAR: 7G; PROTEIN: 12G; SODIUM: 1143MG

CHICKPEA AND COCONUT-CURRY SOUP

Prep time: 10 minutes • **Sauté:** 5 minutes • **Pressure cook:** 10 minutes
Pressure: high • **Release:** quick

Unless you prepare Asian dishes on a regular basis, this soup may require a trip to the store. But I guarantee it's worth it. And don't worry about ingredients going to waste, as there are other recipes in this cookbook that use them all. This soup checks all the boxes for spicy, tart, and savory, and when Carnivorous Maximus tried it for the first time, he remarked it was light but completely satisfying. I agree. **SERVES 4**

Dairy-free • **Nut-free** • **Vegan**
Gluten-free: Replace naan or pita with cooked rice

1 tablespoon olive oil

½ small red onion, thinly sliced

3 tablespoons green curry paste

1 tablespoon chili paste

1 teaspoon kosher salt

1 (14-ounce) can regular or light coconut milk

1 cup vegetable broth or water

2 cups chopped cauliflower or 1 (16-ounce) bag frozen florets

1 (15-ounce) can chickpeas, drained and rinsed

¼ cup jarred sun-dried tomatoes, cut lengthwise into thin strips

1 tablespoon freshly squeezed lime juice

Naan or pita bread, for serving

1. Select the sauté function on the pressure cooker. When the inner cooking pot is warm, heat the olive oil. Add the red onion, curry paste, chili paste, and salt, and cook until the onion softens, 3 to 5 minutes. Add the coconut milk, broth, cauliflower, chickpeas, sun-dried tomatoes, and lime juice.

2. Lock the lid in place. Select the soup function, if your pressure cooker has one, or cook on high pressure for 10 minutes.

3. When the cooking is complete, quick release the pressure. Unlock and remove the lid.

4. Serve with naan or pita bread.

MAKE IT SLOWER: Add all of the ingredients, except the olive oil, to a slow cooker and cook on low for 5 to 6 hours.

PER SERVING: CALORIES: 483; TOTAL FAT: 34G; TOTAL CARBS: 38G; FIBER: 10G; SUGAR: 11G; PROTEIN: 12G; SODIUM: 1278MG

HEARTY MINESTRONE WITH TORTELLINI

Prep time: 10 minutes • **Pressure cook:** 10 minutes
Pressure: high • **Release:** quick

Minestrone is a play on the Italian word for soup, *minestra*, and was likely born of a need to use fresh vegetable pieces left over from previous meals. There's no set recipe, and in fact this hearty soup changes through the year to take advantage of seasonal vegetables that can be pulled together into a comforting, warm broth. But any true minestrone always has some kind of white bean and pasta to turn it into a filling meal. If you'd rather not cook tortellini, I recommend replacing it with 2 cups of uncooked ditalini pasta, a favorite of kids and adults alike. I like to serve this soup with a dollop of fresh pesto. **SERVES 6**

Nut-free

4 cups vegetable broth or water

1 (28-ounce) can crushed tomatoes

2 (15-ounce) cans cannellini beans, drained

2 cups chopped cauliflower

3 celery stalks, sliced

1 cup (1-inch-long) green beans

1 zucchini, diced

1 carrot, sliced

½ yellow onion, diced

1 tablespoon garlic paste or chopped garlic

1 teaspoon kosher salt

1 teaspoon dried oregano

½ teaspoon freshly ground black pepper

2 cups cheese-filled tortellini

1. Add all of the ingredients, except the tortellini, to the inner cooking pot of a pressure cooker.

2. Lock the lid in place. Select the soup setting, if your pressure cooker has one, or cook on high pressure for 10 minutes.

3. While the minestrone is cooking, bring a large pot of water to a boil and cook the tortellini according to the package directions. (If you're on the run, eliminate the pasta and skip this step.)

4. When cooking is complete, quick release the pressure. Unlock and remove the lid.

5. Place ⅓ cup of the cooked tortellini at the bottom of each soup bowl and ladle the soup over it.

MAKE IT SLOWER: Place all of the ingredients, except the pasta, into a slow cooker. Cover and cook on high for 3 to 4 hours or low for 6 to 8 hours. Add the pasta to the slow cooker in the last 30 minutes. For a longer slow cook, switch out the canned beans for dried, and add an additional 2 cups of water or broth. Cook on low for 8 to 10 hours.

MAKE IT AHEAD: This soup freezes well without the pasta.

PER SERVING: CALORIES: 341; TOTAL FAT: 4G; TOTAL CARBS: 59G; FIBER: 13G; SUGAR: 13G; PROTEIN: 19G; SODIUM: 1503MG

BUFFALO CAULIFLOWER CHILI

Prep time: 15 minutes • **Pressure cook:** 15 minutes
Pressure: high • **Release:** 2 minutes natural, then quick

Buffalo wing sauce originated in Buffalo, New York, as a spicy sauce for frying chicken wings. This simple mixture of hot sauce plus melted butter with a pinch of cayenne pepper isn't as über-spicy as it sounds and can be used for everything from grilled shrimp (or tofu) to this soup. Several companies make the sauce, or you can whip up your own batch. The ratio of ingredients is up to you, but I use ½ cup melted unsalted butter with ¾ cup hot sauce. **SERVES 4**

Gluten-free • Nut-free

½ medium cauliflower, cut into bite-size pieces, or 1 (16-ounce) package frozen florets

3 cups vegetable broth

2 (15-ounce) cans cannellini beans, drained

1 (14-ounce) can fire-roasted diced tomatoes with their juices

3 celery stalks, diced

1 medium yellow onion, diced

⅓ cup ranch dressing

¼ cup buffalo wing sauce

2 tablespoons brown sugar

½ teaspoon kosher salt

OPTIONAL TOPPINGS

Blue cheese

Sliced scallions

Tortilla chips

1. Place the cauliflower pieces into the inner cooking pot of the pressure cooker. Add the rest of the ingredients.

2. Lock the lid in place. Select the soup function if your pressure cooker has one, or cook on high pressure for 15 minutes.

3. When cooking is complete, natural release the pressure for 2 minutes, then quick release the remaining pressure. Unlock and remove the lid.

4. Serve with the optional toppings of your choice.

MAKE IT SLOWER: Pile everything into the slow cooker and cook on low for 8 hours.

FLEXITARIAN TIP: Add 2 to 3 cups shredded roasted chicken to the chili along with 1 cup of vegetable broth at the end of cooking. Or cube 2 raw chicken breasts and add them to the inner pot in step 1.

PER SERVING: CALORIES: 238; TOTAL FAT: 2G; TOTAL CARBS: 42G; FIBER: 12G; SUGAR: 14G; PROTEIN: 15G; SODIUM: 1633MG

SOUTHWEST QUINOA CHILI NON CARNE

Prep time: 10 minutes • **Sauté:** 3 minutes • **Pressure cook:** 15 minutes
Pressure: high • **Release:** quick

Quinoa has a natural coating, called saponin, which can have a slightly bitter and soapy flavor. Experts always suggest that home cooks rinse and rub the seeds to remove the coating. My personal rule is if the quinoa will be the main star, as in a quinoa pilaf, I rinse it. But when adding it to a soup, like this chili, I sometimes skip the rinse. Eliminating rinsing saves prep time, and I don't have to wash out a strainer. To finish the chili, select your favorites from a variety of topping options: diced avocado, pickled jalapeños, chopped red onion, sliced scallions, sour cream, and shredded cheese. **SERVES 6**

Gluten-free • Nut-free

2 teaspoons olive oil

1 large onion, diced

2 bell peppers (any color), chopped

1 (28-ounce) can diced tomatoes with their juices

2 cups vegetable broth or water

2 (15-ounce) cans black beans, drained and rinsed

½ cup cooked or frozen quinoa

1 cup fresh or frozen corn

2 tablespoons chili powder

1 tablespoon freshly squeezed lime juice

2 teaspoons garlic paste or minced garlic

1 teaspoon dried oregano

1½ teaspoons kosher salt

½ teaspoon red pepper flakes

1. Select the sauté function on your pressure cooker. Warm the olive oil in the inner cooking pot, then add the onion and bell peppers. Cook for 3 minutes, or until softened.

2. Stir in all of the remaining ingredients.

3. Lock the lid in place. Select the stew function, if your pressure cooker has one, or cook on high pressure for 15 minutes. When cooking is complete, quick release the pressure.

4. Unlock and remove the lid. Taste and adjust for seasoning, if needed.

5. Ladle the chili into individual bowls, and finish with your preferred toppings.

MAKE IT SLOWER: Place all of ingredients except the olive oil in the slow cooker. Cook on high for 3 to 4 hours or low for 6 to 8 hours. If your slow cooker has an aluminum insert, increase the flavor of this chili by cooking the onion and bell peppers in the olive oil on the stove before placing them in the slow cooker.

PER SERVING: CALORIES: 238; TOTAL FAT: 3G; TOTAL CARBS: 43G; FIBER: 11G; SUGAR: 6G; PROTEIN: 13G; SODIUM: 954MG

CORN CHOWDER

Prep time: 15 minutes • **Sauté:** 5 minutes • **Pressure cook:** 10 minutes
Pressure: high • **Release:** quick

There are several ways to thicken soups and sauces, and corn flour works much the same way as cornstarch, but you need much less of it. To thicken up this soup, first stir in one tablespoon of corn flour and allow it to thicken over a couple of minutes before deciding to add the other tablespoon. Best of all, it's gluten-free. **SERVES 4**

Gluten-free • Nut-free

2 tablespoons unsalted butter

1 large yellow onion, diced

1 teaspoon dried oregano

½ teaspoon garlic powder

4 red potatoes, cubed

3 ears corn, kernels sliced off the cob, or 1 (16-ounce) package frozen corn kernels

3 cups vegetable broth

½ teaspoon kosher salt

¼ teaspoon freshly ground black pepper

1 cup heavy (whipping) cream

1 to 2 tablespoons corn flour

8 fresh basil leaves, thinly sliced, or 1 teaspoon store-bought basil paste

1. Select the sauté function on your pressure cooker. Melt the butter in the inner cooking pot. Add the onion, oregano, and garlic powder. Cook, stirring frequently, until the onion becomes translucent and limp, 2 to 3 minutes. Stir in the potatoes, corn, broth, salt, and pepper.

2. Lock the lid in place. Cook on high pressure for 10 minutes. When cooking is complete, quick release the pressure.

3. Unlock and remove the lid. Select the sauté function and stir in the cream and 1 tablespoon of corn flour. Bring to a simmer and cook until slightly thickened, about 1 minute. Stir in the additional 1 tablespoon of corn flour if the soup is thinner than you like. Taste and season with additional salt and pepper, if needed. Top with the basil.

MAKE IT SLOWER: Use ½ teaspoon of onion powder in place of the onion and add it to a slow cooker with the oregano, garlic powder, potatoes, corn, broth, salt, and pepper. Cover and cook on high for 3 to 4 hours or low for 7 to 8 hours. Stir in the butter, cream, and corn flour. Top with the basil.

PER SERVING: CALORIES: 505; TOTAL FAT: 30G; TOTAL CARBS: 52G; FIBER: 6G; SUGAR: 6G; PROTEIN: 11G; SODIUM: 909MG

TOMATO BIRYANI

Prep time: 10 minutes • **Sauté:** 7 minutes • **Pressure cook:** 6 minutes
Pressure: high • **Release:** 10 minutes natural, then quick

No matter where you are in India, you're never far from an aromatic plate of biryani. Biryani shops dot most cities across the country, their signature dishes featuring exotic spices and ingredients unique to that region. Simply described, biryani includes long-grained basmati rice, a long list of spices, vegetables, and usually some kind of meat. They're all placed in a tightly sealed pot, and cooked over a low flame in the steam of their own juices. In this vegetarian version, I've added some water and just enough vegetables and spices to connect you to the soul of this dish. **SERVES 4**

Dairy-free • **Gluten-free** • **Nut-free** • **Vegan**

2 tablespoons olive oil

2 (3-inch) cinnamon sticks

1 teaspoon garam masala

1 teaspoon kosher salt

1 teaspoon jarred or fresh
  grated ginger

2 teaspoons garlic paste
  or minced garlic

1 cup white basmati rice or other
  long-grain rice

1 small red onion, thinly sliced

2 jalapeño peppers, seeded and
  finely diced

1 (14.5-ounce) can diced
  tomatoes with their juices

1½ cups vegetable broth

1. Select the sauté function on your pressure cooker. In the inner cooking pot, heat the olive oil. Add the cinnamon sticks, garam masala, salt, ginger, and garlic. Sauté for 2 minutes, stirring constantly. Add the rice, onion, and jalapeños, and sauté, stirring constantly, for 5 minutes. Add the tomatoes and broth.

2. Lock the lid in place. Cook on high pressure for 6 minutes.

3. When cooking is complete, naturally release the pressure for 10 minutes, then quick release any remaining pressure.

4. Serve as a main dish or side.

PER SERVING: CALORIES: 307; TOTAL FAT: 8G; TOTAL CARBS: 55G; FIBER: 6G; SUGAR: 1G; PROTEIN: 5G; SODIUM: 585MG

ASPARAGUS AND PEA RISOTTO

Prep time: 10 minutes • **Sauté:** 9 minutes • **Pressure cook:** 6 minutes
Pressure: high • **Release:** 5 minutes natural, then quick

I've labored over risottos on the stove, carefully ladling in hot broth, a bit at a time, and stirring endlessly while it's absorbed, before ladling in more broth. I've baked it, which was surprisingly successful, and I've made it in a slow cooker. But making risotto in a pressure cooker is pure genius, as it creates just the right moist sauna for cooking. I guarantee it will be the creamiest, easiest risotto you'll ever make. **SERVES 6**

Gluten-free • Nut-free

¼ cup unsalted butter

1 cup chopped yellow onion

1 bundle asparagus, trimmed
  and cut on the diagonal into
  1½-inch pieces, divided

1½ cups risotto rice, such
  as Arborio

¼ cup white wine

4 cups vegetable broth

¾ teaspoon kosher salt

¼ teaspoon ground black pepper

1 cup frozen peas, thawed

½ cup grated Parmesan cheese

¼ cup Italian parsley,
  coarsely chopped

1. Select the sauté function on an electric pressure cooker. Melt the butter in the inner cooking pot, and stir in the onion. Sauté for 3 minutes, until slightly softened.

2. Stir ¾ cup of the asparagus and all of the rice into the pot, and toss to completely coat.

3. Sauté for 2 minutes, and pour in the wine. Simmer for 3 minutes.

4. Pour in the vegetable broth, salt, and pepper, stirring to scrape the sides of the pot. Simmer for 1 minute.

5. Lock the lid in place. Cook on high pressure for 6 minutes.

6. When the cooking is complete, allow a natural release for 5 minutes, and then perform a quick release. Remove the lid.

7. The risotto will have a layer of liquid on top. Add the remaining asparagus, the peas, and Parmesan cheese, and stir with a large spoon for about 30 seconds until creamy.

8. Serve immediately, topped with the parsley.

MAKE IT SLOWER: To use the slow cooker instead, melt the butter, and combine with the rice in the slow cooker to completely coat. Add the onion, wine, broth, salt, and pepper, and stir. Cook on low for 2½ hours, then add the asparagus and peas. Cook for 30 more minutes, and stir in the Parmesan cheese until creamy. Top with the parsley.

PER SERVING: CALORIES: 335; TOTAL FAT: 10G; TOTAL CARBS: 50G; FIBER: 4G; SUGAR: 4G; PROTEIN: 9G; SODIUM: 814MG

BALSAMIC ROASTED TOMATOES (PAGE 168)

8

KITCHEN STAPLES

BALSAMIC ROASTED TOMATOES

Prep time: 10 minutes • **Cook time:** 4 hours

These little morsels never last long in our kitchen. They add a little burst of umami when added to vegetable and grain dishes, or when tucked inside a grilled cheese sandwich. You can hurry them a bit in the oven by using cherry tomatoes instead of full-size tomatoes, but a slow roast yields the "meatiest" tomatoes. They'll keep in the refrigerator, topped with oil, for at least one month. **MAKES 6 TOMATOES OR 1 PINT OF CHERRY TOMATOES**

Dairy-free • **Gluten-free** • **Nut-free** • **Vegan**

6 medium tomatoes or 1 pint cherry tomatoes

¼ cup, plus 1 tablespoon olive oil

Kosher salt

Freshly ground black pepper

2 teaspoons balsamic vinegar

1. Preheat the oven to 300°F. Line a rimmed baking sheet with parchment paper.

2. Wash and dry the tomatoes, and halve them crosswise. Place them cut-side up on the parchment paper, and drizzle them with ¼ cup of olive oil, allowing the oil to pool on the parchment paper. Sprinkle with the salt and pepper.

3. Roast for 3 to 4 hours, or until the edges of the tomatoes are puckered and the cut surface is a little dry.

4. Drizzle with the balsamic vinegar and let cool on the baking sheet.

5. Pack into an airtight container, and pour any excess oil from the parchment paper on top. Add the remaining 1 tablespoon of oil to the container. Seal and refrigerate for up to one month.

PER SERVING (1 MEDIUM TOMATO): CALORIES: 123; TOTAL FAT: 12G; TOTAL CARBS: 5G; FIBER: 2G; SUGAR: 3G; PROTEIN: 1G; SODIUM: 33MG

CRISPY SPICY CHICKPEAS

Prep time: 5 minutes • **Cook time:** 30 minutes

Perfect as a snack or for garnishing almost anything, these crispy explosions of flavor add an umami taste to many dishes that suggests the smoke and salt of bacon. Try them with roasted Brussels sprouts or a warm spinach salad and you'll see what I mean. Take some on the go for an easy and delicious snack. **MAKES 1 CUP**

Dairy-free • **Gluten-free** • **Nut-free** • **Vegan**

1 cup canned chickpeas, drained and rinsed

1 tablespoon olive oil

½ teaspoon kosher salt

⅛ teaspoon freshly ground black pepper

½ teaspoon smoked paprika

⅛ teaspoon cayenne pepper

1. Preheat the oven to 400°F.

2. Remove any remaining moisture from the chickpeas by rolling them between two paper towels. Place in a medium bowl.

3. Add the olive oil, salt, and pepper to the bowl and toss to completely coat the chickpeas.

4. Spread them out on a baking sheet. Roast for 20 minutes, stir, and roast for an additional 10 minutes, or until lightly crisped.

5. While still warm, toss the chickpeas with the smoked paprika and cayenne pepper. Adding the spices last prevents them from charring in the oven and provides a crispier chickpea.

6. Store at room temperature in an open container for several days. This keeps them crisper longer, although they'll start to lose some crispness over time. They can also be stored in the refrigerator once they've completely cooled.

INGREDIENT TIP: Removing the skins from the chickpeas before baking can improve their crispiness, allowing them to stay crisp for up to two weeks. The easiest way to remove the skins is to lay the chickpeas on a clean dishtowel and lightly salt them. Drape another towel over the chickpeas, and gently rub them against each other. The dishtowels and salt provide the friction necessary for removing the skins.

SUBSTITUTION TIP: Have some fun with the spices you use. Try curry powder, chili powder, garam masala, or some of your own favorite spices and blends.

PER SERVING (¼ CUP): CALORIES: 101; TOTAL FAT: 4G; TOTAL CARBS: 14G; FIBER: 3G; SUGAR: 0G; PROTEIN: 3G; SODIUM: 470MG

ROASTED PUMPKIN SEEDS

Prep time: 5 minutes · **Cook time:** 10 minutes

Roasted pumpkin seeds are a handy garnish for pasta dishes and salads, as well as a healthy snack. Use pumpkin seeds purchased from your market, as long as they're unsalted, or scoop out seeds from a pumpkin you carve or roast. If you use seeds from a raw pumpkin, place the seeds in a bowl of water first to help remove the stringy pulp. Dry them overnight before roasting. **MAKES 1 CUP**

Dairy-free · **Gluten-free** · **Nut-free** · **Vegan**

1 cup unsalted pumpkin seeds

1 teaspoon olive oil

¼ teaspoon kosher salt

Pinch cayenne pepper

Pinch smoked paprika

1. In a small bowl, combine all of the ingredients.

2. Heat a small sauté pan over medium-low heat. Add the pumpkin seeds and sauté, tossing frequently as they brown, for 10 minutes, or until they reach your preferred level of toasting.

3. Cool and store at room temperature in an airtight container for up to two months or in the refrigerator for up to one year.

COOKING TIP: These can also be roasted in a preheated 350°F oven. Once the seeds are coated with the oil and spices, spread them in an even layer on a baking sheet, and roast for about 30 minutes. Stir them occasionally to ensure they brown evenly.

SUBSTITUTION TIP: This recipe also works well for toasting pine nuts in a skillet.

PER SERVING (1 TABLESPOON): CALORIES: 20; TOTAL FAT: 1G; TOTAL CARBS: 2G; FIBER: 0G; SUGAR: 0G; PROTEIN: 1G; SODIUM: 36MG

LEMONY BREADCRUMBS

Prep time: 2 minutes • **Cook time:** 5 minutes

I make these breadcrumbs 2 cups at a time and keep them stored in the refrigerator. They take less than 10 minutes to make, if starting with store-bought breadcrumbs, and are ready at a moment's notice for adding a bright crunch to salads, vegetables, and grain dishes. **MAKES 1 CUP**

Dairy-free • Nut-free • Vegan

2 teaspoons olive oil

1 cup panko

⅛ teaspoon kosher salt

⅛ teaspoon freshly ground black pepper

Zest of 1 lemon (about ½ teaspoon or more, to taste)

1. In a small skillet over medium heat, warm the olive oil. Add the panko, salt, and pepper. Toss to lightly coat, and toast until the breadcrumbs are a golden color, about 3 minutes. You'll need to stir the breadcrumbs about every 30 seconds so they toast evenly.

2. Remove from the heat, and stir in the lemon zest.

3. Transfer to a plate to cool before storing in an airtight container.

INGREDIENT TIP: If you prefer to use fresh breadcrumbs, pulse two or three slices of dry, day-old bread in a food processor until large crumbs form. If the bread is fresh, dry it in a preheated 300°F oven for 10 to 15 minutes before preparing this recipe.

MAKE IT AHEAD: These breadcrumbs will stay fresh for three to four weeks in a sealed jar in the refrigerator, or up to six months in the freezer.

PER SERVING (2 TABLESPOONS): CALORIES: 63; TOTAL FAT: 2G; TOTAL CARBS: 10G; FIBER: 1G; SUGAR: 1G; PROTEIN: 2G; SODIUM: 134MG

LEMONY MOROCCAN CHERMOULA SAUCE

Prep time: 10 minutes

Think of this as Morocco's answer to Italy's pesto, but without the cheese. A coarse paste of fresh olive oil, herbs, garlic, lemon, and aromatic spices, chermoula adds a flavor burst to vegetable dishes like broccoli, asparagus, and potatoes, and brightens grain dishes. It's also a perfect tincture of herbs on scrambled eggs, in soups, or on a salad. **MAKES ¼ CUP**

Dairy-free · **Gluten-free** · **Nut-free** · **Vegan**

¼ cup fresh cilantro, finely chopped

¼ cup fresh parsley, finely chopped

¼ cup fresh mint, finely chopped

3 tablespoons extra-virgin olive oil

1 tablespoon freshly squeezed lemon juice

½ teaspoon garlic paste or minced garlic

½ teaspoon smoked paprika

⅛ teaspoon kosher salt

1. In a small bowl, mix together all of the ingredients.

2. Store in an airtight container in the refrigerator for up to two weeks, or in the freezer for up to six months.

MAKE IT AHEAD: Quadruple the recipe to make 1 cup of sauce, and scoop it into an ice cube tray sprayed with olive oil. Freeze, pop out the cubes into a freezer bag, and store for up to six months.

INGREDIENT TIP: Fresh herbs don't always last long before wilting. I often use herbs that come in a tube for this sauce, such as Gourmet Garden products. They last much longer and allow this sauce to come together very quickly. Find them in the fresh produce section of your local market.

PER SERVING (1 TABLESPOON): CALORIES: 100; TOTAL FAT: 11G; TOTAL CARBS: 2G; FIBER: 1G; SUGAR: 0G; PROTEIN: 1G; SODIUM: 79MG

How to Make Garlic Paste

I purchase garlic paste in tubes at my local grocery, but inevitably there are times when I need to make my own. All I need are a few garlic cloves, a chef's knife, cutting board, and salt to make 1 tablespoon of paste.

1. Place 4 large garlic cloves on a cutting board, and lay the flat side of a chef's knife on top of them. Smack sharply on the knife to smash the garlic and pop off their skins.

2. Finely chop the cloves and sprinkle them with ¼ teaspoon of kosher salt. Gather into a pile and thoroughly mince.

3. Scrape the minced garlic into a paste by working the sharp edge of the knife, at a slight angle, in a scraping–smashing motion until a paste develops.

4. Alternatively, place the minced garlic in the bowl of a mortar and pestle set, and grind the garlic into a paste.

Garlic paste keeps in the refrigerator in a sealed container for a few days, although it's best the day you make it. Or transfer the paste to an ice cube tray sprayed with olive oil. Freeze, pop out the cubes, and store in a freezer bag for up to six months.

For roasted garlic paste, slice off the top third of a head of garlic to expose the cloves. Drizzle the cut top with a little olive oil and wrap the head in aluminum foil. Roast in a preheated 350°F oven for 1 hour. Pinch the garlic from the skins, and smash into a paste with a little salt.

MISO BUTTER

Prep time: 5 minutes

Sometimes fabulous flavor comes from something so easy, you wonder why you haven't used it forever. This barely-a-recipe qualifies as one of those things. Toss this with almost any vegetable or grain for a big oomph of umami, and you'll see what I mean. It will keep in the refrigerator for up to six months, but I guarantee you'll use it up way before then. **MAKES ½ CUP**

Nut-free
Gluten-free: Use gluten-free miso

4 tablespoons white miso

4 tablespoons unsalted butter, at room temperature

In a small bowl, thoroughly mash together the miso and butter using a fork. Store in the refrigerator in a small airtight container.

INGREDIENT TIP: Some miso products are gluten-free, but many are not. It's best to check the labels. Gluten-free miso products are identified as such.

PER SERVING (1 TABLESPOON): CALORIES: 68; TOTAL FAT: 6G; TOTAL CARBS: 2G; FIBER: 1G; SUGAR: 1G; PROTEIN: 1G; SODIUM: 361MG

TZATZIKI

Prep time: 15 minutes, plus 1 hour to chill

This garlicky yogurt sauce is packed with grated cucumber and fresh herbs, and is popular in many regions of the world. It is a perfect condiment for spicy food. India calls its version *raita*, and there's a Turkish version known as *cacik*. Tzatziki is Greece's contribution to the mix. It tastes best the day it's made but can last a day or two in the refrigerator before it becomes too watery from the cucumber. **MAKES 1½ CUPS**

Gluten-free • Nut-free

1 cup plain Greek yogurt

1 medium cucumber, peeled, seeded, grated, and drained

1 tablespoon extra-virgin olive oil

1 tablespoon freshly squeezed lemon juice

1 teaspoon kosher salt

1 teaspoon garlic paste or minced garlic

1 teaspoon chopped fresh dill

1 teaspoon chopped fresh mint

1 teaspoon freshly ground black pepper

In a small bowl, combine all of the ingredients. Refrigerate for 1 hour to allow the flavors to develop.

PER SERVING (2 TABLESPOONS): CALORIES: 28; TOTAL FAT: 2G; TOTAL CARBS: 2G; FIBER: 0G; SUGAR: 1G; PROTEIN: 2G; SODIUM: 203MG

SMOOTH AND CREAMY HUMMUS

Prep time: 10 minutes • **Cook time:** 10 minutes

The surprise ingredient in a smooth and creamy hummus is a little baking soda, which breaks the chickpeas apart. After processing the chickpeas, you'll have a hummus as luscious as buttercream frosting. **MAKES 1¾ CUPS**

Dairy-free • Gluten-free • Nut-free • Vegan

1½ cups canned chickpeas, drained and rinsed

½ teaspoon baking soda

⅓ cup tahini

2 tablespoons freshly squeezed lemon juice, plus more to taste

1 teaspoon garlic paste or minced garlic

½ teaspoon smoked paprika, plus more to taste

½ teaspoon kosher salt, plus more to taste

½ teaspoon freshly ground black pepper

2 to 4 tablespoons cold water

Extra-virgin olive oil, for serving

1. Place the chickpeas in a medium pot over medium heat and pour in enough water to cover them by about 2 inches. Add the baking soda. Bring to a boil, reduce the heat to a simmer, and cook until the chickpeas begin to break apart, 7 to 9 minutes. Drain and place in the bowl of a food processor.

2. Add the tahini, lemon juice, garlic paste, paprika, salt, and pepper. Process until a smooth paste develops.

3. Add the water, 1 tablespoon at a time, until the hummus achieves the consistency you prefer. You will need to stop the processor a few times to scrape down the sides of the bowl.

4. Season to taste with additional salt, lemon juice, and paprika.

5. Serve with a drizzle of olive oil.

PER SERVING (¼ CUP): CALORIES: 128; TOTAL FAT: 7G; TOTAL CARBS: 13G; FIBER: 4G; SUGAR: 2G; PROTEIN: 5G; SODIUM: 274MG

EASY ROASTED RED PEPPER AIOLI

Prep time: 10 minutes · **Cook time:** 20 minutes

This versatile sauce comes together quickly since most of the time is spent with the peppers roasting in the oven while you throw in a load of laundry and answer a few emails. The remaining work is done by your food processor or blender. This sauce keeps in the refrigerator for a few days and can be used as a veggie dip, a spread on your next grilled cheese sandwich, or a little something extra in a warm grain dish. **MAKES ⅔ CUP**

Dairy-free · Gluten-free · Nut-free

2 large red bell peppers

8 oil-packed sun-dried tomatoes, with their oil

2 large egg yolks

2 tablespoons Dijon mustard

2 teaspoons freshly squeezed lemon juice

¼ cup extra-virgin olive oil

Pinch salt (optional)

1. Preheat the oven to 450°F. Line a baking sheet with aluminum foil or parchment paper.

2. Place the red peppers on the baking sheet and roast for 20 minutes, or until blackened and soft. Turn the peppers every 5 minutes for an even roast.

3. Wrap the roasted peppers in aluminum foil for about 5 minutes to loosen the skin. Once cool enough to handle, peel and seed the peppers, and coarsely chop them.

4. Place the roasted peppers, sun-dried tomatoes, egg yolks, mustard, and lemon juice into the bowl of a food processor fitted with a metal blade. Pulse a few times to pull the sauce together.

5. With the food processor running, drizzle the olive oil into the sauce. Continue processing until the sauce is thick and smooth.

6. Add the salt, if needed.

INGREDIENT TIP: Use pasteurized eggs for the raw egg yolks if there is a health concern.

SUBSTITUTION TIP: Use 3 large jarred roasted red peppers in place of the red bell peppers. Dry them with a paper towel before using.

PER SERVING (1 TABLESPOON): CALORIES: 55; TOTAL FAT: 5G; TOTAL CARBS: 2G; FIBER: 1G; SUGAR: 1G; PROTEIN: 1G; SODIUM: 43MG

LIME VINAIGRETTE

Prep time: 10 minutes

This quick vinaigrette sharpens salads that contain black beans or pinto beans while infusing them with a hint of smoke. I keep it handy on the counter, where it lasts for four to five days. If you refrigerate it in a sealed jar, it will keep for a couple of weeks without losing its freshness. **MAKES ¼ CUP**

Dairy-free · **Gluten-free** · **Nut-free**
Vegan: Use agave nectar or granulated sugar instead of honey

1 tablespoon freshly squeezed lime juice

1 tablespoon extra-virgin olive oil

½ tablespoon white wine vinegar

½ teaspoon honey

¼ teaspoon ancho chile powder

¼ teaspoon kosher salt

In a small bowl, whisk together all of the ingredients. Store in an airtight container on the counter for up to five days or refrigerate for up to two weeks.

SUBSTITUTION TIP: To make a lemon vinaigrette, swap out lime juice for lemon juice and exchange the ancho chile powder for garlic powder.

PER SERVING (2 TABLESPOONS): CALORIES: 68; TOTAL FAT: 7G; TOTAL CARBS: 2G; FIBER: 0G; SUGAR: 2G; PROTEIN: 0G; SODIUM: 320MG

TAHINI MISO DRESSING

Prep time: 10 minutes

This dressing can be modified with great ease to your personal tastes and can be made in a bowl using a spoon or whisk, or with a food processor. It will keep for months in the refrigerator and needs only a quick stir if the liquid has separated out. **MAKES ¾ CUP**

Dairy-free • **Vegan**
Gluten-free: Use gluten-free tamari and gluten-free miso

¼ cup tahini

1 tablespoon tamari or low-sodium soy sauce

1 tablespoon white miso

1 tablespoon freshly squeezed lemon juice

1 tablespoon maple syrup or honey

¼ cup warm water

Freshly ground black pepper

In a small bowl, whisk the tahini, tamari, miso, lemon juice, and maple syrup together. Whisk in the water and black pepper. Store in an airtight container in the refrigerator for up to six months.

MODIFICATION TIP: To further simplify this dressing, eliminate the tamari and sweetener. Both versions work very well in vegetable and grain salads.

PER SERVING (2 TABLESPOONS): CALORIES: 76; TOTAL FAT: 6G; TOTAL CARBS: 5G; FIBER: 1G; SUGAR: 2G; PROTEIN: 2G; SODIUM: 287MG

MEASUREMENTS AND CONVERSIONS

VOLUME EQUIVALENTS (LIQUID)

US STANDARD	US STANDARD (OUNCES)	METRIC (APPROXIMATE)
2 tablespoons	1 fl. oz.	30 mL
¼ cup	2 fl. oz.	60 mL
½ cup	4 fl. oz.	120 mL
1 cup	8 fl. oz.	240 mL
1½ cups	12 fl. oz.	355 mL
2 cups or 1 pint	16 fl. oz.	475 mL
4 cups or 1 quart	32 fl. oz.	1 L
1 gallon	128 fl. oz.	4 L

OVEN TEMPERATURES

FAHRENHEIT (F)	CELSIUS (C) (APPROXIMATE)
250°F	120°C
300°F	150°C
325°F	165°C
350°F	180°C
375°F	190°C
400°F	200°C
425°F	220°C
450°F	230°C

VOLUME EQUIVALENTS (DRY)

US STANDARD	METRIC (APPROXIMATE)
⅛ teaspoon	0.5 mL
¼ teaspoon	1 mL
½ teaspoon	2 mL
¾ teaspoon	4 mL
1 teaspoon	5 mL
1 tablespoon	15 mL
¼ cup	59 mL
⅓ cup	79 mL
½ cup	118 mL
⅔ cup	156 mL
¾ cup	177 mL
1 cup	235 mL
2 cups or 1 pint	475 mL
3 cups	700 mL
4 cups or 1 quart	1 L

WEIGHT EQUIVALENTS

US STANDARD	METRIC (APPROXIMATE)
½ ounce	15 g
1 ounce	30 g
2 ounces	60 g
4 ounces	115 g
8 ounces	225 g
12 ounces	340 g
16 ounces or 1 pound	455 g

REFERENCE GUIDE TO PREPPING AND COOKING PRODUCE

VEGGIE / FRUIT	PREPPING OPTIONS	TOOLS
ACORN SQUASH	Slice off stem, halve and remove seeds and pulp, then slice into wedges, purée, or dice	Chef's knife; spoon; food processor or blender
APPLE	Remove stem and core, slice, then purée, spiralize, halve, or dice	Paring knife; food processor or blender; chef's knife; spiralizer; mandoline
ASPARAGUS	Remove bottom third of the stalk, at least, to remove more fibrous ends; peel into ribbons lengthwise, slice into thin disks, or purée	Chef's knife; vegetable peeler; food processor or blender
AVOCADO	Slice in half lengthwise, twist to separate, remove pit using a knife, slice into wedges or chunks, and slide a spoon between the flesh and skin to scoop out; purée or mash	Chef's knife; food processor; mortar and pestle
BASIL, MINT, SAGE	Roll or stack to thinly slice; mash using a mortar and pestle or purée	Chef's knife; food processor; mortar and pestle
BEETS	Slice off ends and peel, chop, or dice; spiralize red beets; purée, peel into ribbons, or grate	Chef's knife; paring knife; vegetable peeler; spiralizer; food processor or blender; box grater
BELL PEPPERS	Place a pepper on a workspace with the stem facing up and slice the side "lobes" and the bottom off, then discard the seeds, pith, and top (which should be all connected as one piece); slice into lengths, dice, or purée	Chef's knife; food processor or blender

RAW / COOKED	COOKING METHODS	SERVING IDEAS
Cooked	Roast; sauté; steam; braise; slow cooker; pressure cooker	Stuffed roasted halves; roasted wedges; soup
Raw / cooked	Roast; sauté; simmer; braise; bake; slow cooker; pressure cooker	Raw snack or dessert; baked into chips; roasted or raw salads; relish; add to puréed soups; applesauce; apple butter; pickled; pie; cake; smoothie; bread; purée and add to a vinaigrette; slaws
Raw / cooked	Roast; steam; sauté; simmer; slow cooker; pressure cooker	Salad; add to pasta, legume, grain, and vegetable dishes; soup; pickled; risotto; anything with eggs, such as quiche
Raw / cooked	Grill; fry	Add to salads, sandwiches, and pasta; guacamole; place wedges on toast and top with olive oil, salt, and pepper; anything with cooked eggs, such as omelets; add to smoothie; use in a sauce or dressing
Raw / cooked	Sauté; roast; simmer	Pesto; add to salads, vegetables, grains, legumes, pasta, and eggs; add to dressings and sauces; add to pizza and breads, such as foccacia
Raw / cooked	Sauté; roast; simmer; steam; bake; slow cooker; pressure cooker	Chilled soup with sour cream and dill; pickled; add to salads, pasta, grain, and vegetable dishes; add purée to breads and chocolate cake batter; ravioli filling or pasta dough; add spiralized noodles to soups or use as pasta noodles; bake as chips; raw slaws; sauté with butter and maple syrup
Raw / cooked	Roast; sauté; simmer; bake; grill; stir-fry; slow cooker; pressure cooker	Roast and peel, slice in half, seed, and drizzle with olive oil, plus capers, garlic, salt, and pepper; purée as soup; add to tomato sauces; stuff whole with grains and vegetables; add to salads, sandwiches, grains, legumes, and pasta; raw with a dip; add to bread; add to a soffritto of onion, celery, and carrots; add to sauces such as aioli

VEGGIE / FRUIT	PREPPING OPTIONS	TOOLS
BOK CHOY	Slice off root end and use whole or chop	Chef's knife
BROCCOLI	Trim fibrous ends and snap off leaves, peel off the outer tough skin, and separate florets by slicing through the stems; slice the stems into batons, thinly slice into disks, chop, or dice	Chef's knife; food processor or blender
BRUSSELS SPROUTS	Trim bottoms and remove any wilted or yellowed leaves, thinly slice, halve, or grate	Chef's knife; food processor fitted with a grater; mandoline
BUTTERNUT SQUASH	Slice off ends, cut the squash in two just above the bulbous end, stand on end, and peel with a sharp knife or vegetable peeler; scoop out seeds with a spoon; slice into wedges, chop, dice, purée, or spiralize	Chef's knife; food processor; blender; spiralizer
CABBAGE	Slice into wedges, thinly slice, or grate	Chef's knife; box grater
CARROT	Trim top, and peel; slice, dice, grate, or peel into ribbons	Chef's knife; paring knife; box grater; vegetable peeler
CAULIFLOWER	Trim bottom and remove leaves; slice into steaks; cut off florets at the stems; chop or dice stems; grate into rice, purée, or mash	Chef's knife; paring knife; box grater; food processor or blender

RAW / COOKED	COOKING METHODS	SERVING IDEAS
Raw / cooked	Braise; grill; sauté; simmer; roast; stir-fry; steam	Warm or raw salad; raw slaws; soup; ramen; add to grain, vegetable, and legume dishes; raw with a dip for an appetizer; pickled; add to a green smoothie
Raw / cooked	Bake; blanch; braise; fry; grill; roast; sauté; simmer; steam; stir-fry; slow cooker; pressure cooker	Add to egg dishes, such as casseroles and quiche; roast with olive oil, smoked paprika, salt, and pepper, and finish with lemon juice; stir-fry with other vegetables in sesame oil, and finish with soy sauce; add to raw salads, Buddha bowls, grains, legumes, and vegetable casseroles; roast and toss with pasta, capers, preserved lemon, grated Parmesan cheese, and toasted breadcrumbs; soup; add roasted broccoli to pizza toppings
Raw / cooked	Roast; bake; steam; braise; fry; sauté; grill; pressure cooker; slow cooker	Slice thinly for a raw salad with green onions and dried cranberries; roast with apples; make a hash with potatoes, onion, and apple cider vinegar; toss with garlic, spices, and olive oil and throw on the grill; bake into a cheesy gratin
Cooked	Roast; sauté; steam; simmer; slow cooker; pressure cooker	Stuff with grains and/or vegetables; spiralize into pasta; add to salads, grains, legumes, and vegetables; soup; risotto
Raw / cooked	Roast; braise; sauté; steam; grill; bake; stir-fry; slow cooker	Roast wedges rubbed with olive oil, garlic paste, salt, and pepper; braise red cabbage with olive oil, cider vinegar, brown sugar, and apple chunks; slaw; cabbage rolls stuffed with rice and vegetables; pickle for kimchi; topping for tacos
Raw / cooked	Roast; braise; sauté; steam; grill; bake; stir-fry; slow cooker; pressure cooker; simmer; steam	Raw in a salad; soup; slaw; soufflé; bread; cake; add to vegetable, grain, and legume dishes; simmer in a pan with butter, honey, and orange juice until all the liquid is gone except a glaze
Raw / cooked	Bake; blanch; braise; fry; grill; roast; sauté; simmer; steam; stir-fry; pressure cooker; slow cooker	Purée into a sauce; grate into rice for tabbouleh or risotto; roast whole, smothered with a spicy sauce; substitute it for chicken in many dishes; soup; pickle for kimchi; swap out potatoes in mashed potatoes; use in a gratin; toss with pasta, lemon, capers, and breadcrumbs

VEGGIE / FRUIT	PREPPING OPTIONS	TOOLS
CELERY	Trim bottoms; slice into long strips or dice	Chef's knife
CORN	Remove kernels by standing a cob up in a bowl lined with a towel. Anchor it with one hand, and slide a knife down the cob to slice off the kernels.	Chef's knife
CUCUMBER	Peel, halve, and scrape out juicy seeds; slice into thin or thick slices, peel into long ribbons, dice, grate, or pickle	Vegetable peeler; chef's knife; paring knife; spoon; box grater
DELICATA SQUASH	Slice off the ends, halve, and scrape out the seeds; slice into half-moons or purée	Chef's knife; spoon; food processor or blender
EGGPLANT	Slice off the ends, slice into ¾-inch slices, sprinkle evenly with salt, lay in a colander to drain for 30 minutes, then rinse to remove the salt and pat dry; slice, chop, dice, mash, or purée	Chef's knife; colander
GARLIC	Peel. Chop the bulbs, thinly slice, mince, or smash and lightly salt to form a paste	Chef's knife
GINGER	Peel with a spoon and trim; slice, mince, or grate	Spoon; paring knife; fine grater or zester
GREEN BEANS	Trim; slice lengthwise or slice crosswise on the diagonal	Paring knife; chef's knife

RAW / COOKED	COOKING METHODS	SERVING IDEAS
Raw / cooked	Roast; braise; sauté; bake; stir-fry; simmer	Use for making stock; soffritto; make a celery gratin; braise in broth with tomatoes and onions, and top with shavings of Parmesan; add to salads for crunch
Raw / cooked	Sauté; roast; simmer; steam; grill	Chowder; stew; add to tacos with black beans, tomatoes, and avocado with a squeeze of lime; sauté with pickled onion, basil, and tomatoes and stuff into peppers with a little cheese; risotto; toss with zoodles, mint, and tomatoes; make Mexican corn
Raw / cooked	Sauté; bake; stir-fry;	Use in salads, especially Greek and Middle Eastern salads; make tzatziki; swap out bread for cucumber disks; pickled; chilled soup; make a sandwich with cream cheese and dill; add slices to jugs of water; sauté with a little butter, salt, pepper, scallions, and mint
Cooked	Roast; bake; sauté; simmer; grill; braise; steam; slow cooker; pressure cooker; stir-fry	Soup; stuff scooped-out half with grains, dried fruits, and other vegetables; drizzle with oil and garlic, sprinkle with salt, pepper, and cayenne, and roast; add to warm salads or Buddha bowls; use as a pizza topping; toss with pasta; add to tacos; purée to add to chilis and stews; bake into a gratin
Cooked	Bake; roast; sauté; simmer; grill; stir-fry; braise; slow cooker; pressure cooker	Mash into a dip such as baba ghanoush; marinate and grill for a sandwich with tomatoes and smoked mozzarella; lightly bread and bake in a tomato sauce topped with Parmesan; roast and stuff with a grains and pomegrante seed salad; simmer with tomatoes, onion, garlic, and balsamic vinegar and puree for a soup
Raw / cooked	Roast; sauté; blanch; bake; stir-fry	Wrap a head of garlic with a drizzle of olive oil and a sprig of rosemary in foil and roast; sauté or roast chopped or thinly sliced garlic with vegetables, legumes, or grains; add to a soup with onions and thyme
Raw / cooked	Simmer; sauté; stir-fry	Tea; add to broths and soups; grate finely to add to fruit with a squeeze of fresh lime; add to miso and garlic paste to rub on vegetables; gingerbread; add to sauces or jams
Cooked	Blanch; sauté; simmer; bake; roast; stir-fry	Add to salads, soups, and grains; roast with olive oil, thyme, salt, pepper, and a squeeze of lemon

VEGGIE / FRUIT	PREPPING OPTIONS	TOOLS
JALAPEÑO PEPPERS, SERRANO CHILES	Trim off the stem, slice in half, and remove the seeds and pith; slice, dice, or mince	Paring knife
KALE	Fold leaves over the central tough rib, and remove the rib with a knife (not necessary for baby kale); coarsely chop	Chef's knife
LEEKS	Cut and discard the top part of the leek with tough, dark green leaves, split in half lengthwise, and feather under cold running water to remove dirt; slice into thin half-moons	Chef's knife
MANGO	Slice "cheeks" of mango off from stem to end, parallel and as close as possible to the long, flat pit; score the cheeks down to, but not through, the skin using the tip of a sharp knife; turn the cheek 90 degrees and score again. Scoop out the mango chunks using a spoon; purée.	Paring knife; food processor or blender
MUSHROOMS, SMALL	Wipe clean with a paper towel and slice, quarter, or mince.	Chef's knife
OLIVES (GREEN, NIÇOISE, KALAMATA)	Slice, smash using the flat side of a chef's knife, coarsely chop, or leave whole	Chef's knife
ONION, SHALLOT	Chop, dice, grate, or slice	Chef's knife
PARSLEY AND CILANTRO	Position a sharp knife at a 45-degree angle to the herbs and slice across the leaves to coarsely chop, including stems; gather the leaves and stems together and chop into smaller pieces or continue chopping to mince	Chef's knife

RAW / COOKED	COOKING METHODS	SERVING IDEAS
Raw / cooked	Sauté; roast; bake; stir-fry	Roast with cornbread batter; roast with cheese; add to vegetable and legume dishes; pickle; add to cheese sandwiches or quesadillas; use in traditional tomato salsas or ones with diced pineapple and mango; jelly
Raw / cooked	Sauté; blanch; bake; roast; stir-fry; simmer; braise; grill; steam	Pesto; baked kale chips; sauté with lemon, olives, and capers, and toss with quinoa; add to soup; braise with garlic, dried chipotle chiles, and tomatoes; add to a green smoothie
Raw / cooked	Sauté; roast	Raw in salads; add to sautéed or roasted vegetables; roast halves in the oven with olive oil, salt, and pepper
Raw	Bake; grill	Smoothie; soup; sauces; relish with bell peppers, black beans, jalapeño, and shallots with a squeeze of lime juice; add to salads; add the purée to pound cake, muffins, pudding, ice cream, or sorbet; dry into fruit leather; spring rolls
Raw / cooked	Sauté; bake; stir-fry; roast; braise; grill	Coat with olive oil and a dusting of salt and pepper and roast at 400°F until well-browned; add to pasta and grain dishes; make mushroom risotto; stuff with peppers, garlic, breadcrumbs, and Parmesan cheese for an appetizer; use in casseroles
Raw / cooked	Sauté; roast	Add to pastas, grains, vegetables, and legumes
Raw / cooked	Bake; braise; fry; grill; roast; sauté; stir-fry; pressure cooker; slow cooker	Stuff sweet onions with grains and other vegetables and roast; caramelize and add to sandwiches, burgers, grains, and legumes; make a flatbread with caramelized onions, ricotta cheese, and herbs
Raw / cooked	Suitable for all kinds of cooking	Add to most vegetable, pasta, grain and legume dishes, including roasts, soups, and casseroles

VEGGIE / FRUIT	PREPPING OPTIONS	TOOLS
PEACHES / NECTARINES	Peel and pit: for freestone peaches and nectarines, slice in half lengthwise, twist the halves apart, and remove pit; for non-freestone varieties, slice the peach from top to bottom, then slice a second time to create a narrow peach wedge, and pry it from the pit using the knife. Slice peach halves into wedges, dice, or purée	Chef's knife; food processor or blender
PEAS	Pry the shells open with your nails or a small knife, and remove the peas; purée or leave whole	Food processor or blender
PORTABELLA MUSHROOMS	Wipe clean with a paper towel, and scrape out the gills using a spoon; leave whole or slice	Chef's knife; spoon
POTATOES, WHITE, RED, YUKON, FINGERLING	Peel (or not), slice, dice, mash, purée, grate, spiralize, or smash	Vegetable peeler; chef's knife; paring knife; potato ricer or masher; box grater; spiralizer; food processor (using pulse only); mandoline
RADISHES	Trim roots and tops; leave whole, halve, or thinly slice	Paring knife
SCALLIONS	Trim roots, and remove any outer damaged sheath; leave whole, slice in half lengthwise, or chop	Paring knife; chef's knife
SUGAR SNAP PEAS, SNOW PEAS	Trim ends and leave whole or thinly slice	Paring knife; chef's knife
SPAGHETTI SQUASH	Cut in half or leave whole; scoop out seeds and pulp with a spoon; after cooking, run the tines of a fork across the flesh to pull up "spaghetti" strands	Chef's knife; spoon; fork
SPINACH	Stack leaves, remove stems (not necessary for baby spinach), roll into a fat cigar shape, and thinly slice; gather slices together and mince	Chef's knife

RAW / COOKED	COOKING METHODS	SERVING IDEAS
Raw / cooked	Bake; braise; grill; roast; sauté	Smoothies; soup; sauces; baste in butter, brown sugar, and cinnamon and grill; add raw peach slices to salads and grain dishes; make peach ice cream
Raw / cooked	Bake; blanch; braise; sauté; simmer; steam; stir-fry	Add to pasta, casseroles, soup, and vegetable dishes; purée for a pea soup; lightly sauté with salt and pepper, and toss with mint; add to an asparagus quiche or omelet
Raw / cooked	Grill; roast; sauté; braise; bake	Use in place of a bun for veggie burgers; stuff with vegetables, grains, or legumes; marinate in olive oil, balsamic vinegar, and garlic and roast or grill
Cooked	Bake; braise; fry; grill; pressure cooker; roast; sauté; simmer; slow cooker; steam; stir-fry	Twice-baked potatoes whipped with soft cheese topped with chives; spiralize and toss with olive oil, salt, and pepper, and roast until browned; grill slices of potato to add to salads; potato gratin; smash roasted baby red potatoes, sprinkle with salt, pepper, and dried rosemary, and drizzle with olive oil; roast; hash browns
Raw / cooked	Bake; braise; fry; stir-fry	Bake or roast with butter, salt, pepper, and parsley; add to salads
Raw / cooked	Braise; roast; grill; sauté; stir-fry	Toss in olive oil, salt, and pepper and roast or grill; pickle; add to salads, soups, pasta, grains, pizza, or legume dishes; add to any kind of egg dishes
Raw / cooked	Bake; braise; grill; roast; sauté; steam; stir-fry	Toss in olive oil, salt, and pepper and grill, then toss with chopped mint before serving; sauté and sprinkle with sea salt; sauté in sesame oil, and finish with lemon, salt, pepper, and sesame seeds
Cooked	Roast; bake; pressure cook; slow cook	Stuff with black beans, roasted red peppers, and onions, and top with cheese; toss strands with olive oil, Parmesan cheese, salt, pepper, and roasted pumpkin seeds
Raw / cooked	Blanch; braise; sauté; simmer; stir-fry	Sauté in a little olive oil, salt, and pepper, and toss with cooked quinoa, yellow raisins, and a squeeze of lemon; add to soups, salads, sandwiches, and pasta; mince for spanakopita

VEGGIE / FRUIT	PREPPING OPTIONS	TOOLS
STRAWBERRIES	Hull by cutting out the top stem; halve, thinly slice, dice, or purée	Paring knife; food processor or blender
SWEET POTATOES	Peel with a vegetable peeler; slice, dice, chop, grate, spiralize, or purée	Chef's knife; vegetable peeler; spiralizer; food processor or blender; box grater
SWISS CHARD, MUSTARD GREENS, DANDELION GREENS	Remove the central fibrous stem, if applicable, and stack several leaves on top of one another; fold in half lengthwise, roll into a fat cigar shape, and slice crosswise into wide or narrow ribbons; gather ribbons together and finely chop or mince	Chef's knife
TOMATOES	To peel a tomato, score the skin on the bottom of the tomato with an X, blanch in simmering water for 20 seconds, then dip in a bowl of ice water, and peel starting at the X; slice, chop, dice, grate, or purée	Paring knife or chef's knife; box grater; food processor or blender
ZUCCHINI, SUMMER SQUASH	Trim the ends and chop, dice, or slice into rounds, wedges, or matchstick lengths; grate using the largest holes of a box grater; spiralize	Paring knife or chef's knife; box grater; spiralizer; food processor or blender; mandoline

RAW / COOKED	COOKING METHODS	SERVING IDEAS
Raw / cooked	Roast; sauté; grill	Roast and drizzle with balsamic vinegar for a sauce; purée for a sauce or to make ice cream; add to baked goods like cakes, scones, biscuits, and pies; pipe uncooked cheesecake batter into hulled strawberries; dice raw strawberries for salsas
Cooked	Roast; bake; sauté; simmer; grill; steam; slow cooker; pressure cooker	Baked and stuffed; spiralized; purée for a sauce, soup, or to add to pancake batter; add to stews and chili; enchiladas; tacos; season, roast, and add to warm salads and Buddha bowls; add to root vegetable roasts and gratins; baked sweet potato chips; sauté with butter and maple syrup; season and bake sweet potato fries; hash
Raw / cooked	Bake; blanch; braise; roast; sauté; simmer; steam	Use Swiss chard leaves for rolling up grains and vegetables, cover with a pasta sauce and cheese, and bake; sauté Swiss chard stems separately with garlic, salt, and pepper, finished with a vinegar drizzle; sauté garlic and onion, add broth, salt, and pepper, and braise mustard greens until tender; sauté dandelion greens in olive oil, garlic, salt, pepper, and red pepper flakes
Raw / cooked	Bake; blanch; braise; fry; grill; roast; sauté; simmer; stir-fry	Stuff raw with chickpea or lentil salad; slice in half and slow-roast with garlic, salt, and pepper; panzanella bread salad; tomato jam; salsa; Caprese; bruschetta; gazpacho
Raw / cooked	Bake; grill; roast; sauté; simmer; steam; stir-fry	Bake as fries: slice into wedges, toss in olive oil, salt, pepper, oregano, and Parmesan cheese; spiralize for spaghetti, then toss with tomatoes, basil, and garlic; slice in half lengthwise, then slightly hollow out to make boats and stuff with vegetables and grains topped with pasta sauce and cheese

RECIPE INDEX BY MEAL TYPE

ACKNOWLEDGMENTS

Mom, for showing me that cooking is social, from her brunches with neighbors when I was a child, to her multicourse dinners for her wide circle of friends.

Ina, for showing me that cooking is sharing and friendship that lasts a lifetime.

Tante Marie's Cooking School in San Francisco, for showing me that cooking is science, technique, and taste memory.

Food52, for showing me that cooking is creative and fun, and for giving me the confidence to create my own recipes and launch my own food blog. Amanda and Merrill, the supportive community you have created there gave root to my dreams.

My fellow bloggers, who showed me that food was a way to connect to one another, and to develop new virtual friendships that became much more than virtual.

Molly O'Neill, for opening up a world of food writing, growing my food writing vocabulary, and showing me powerful ways to evoke food memories. And to the writing group she formed for sharing our work—I learned so much from each of you.

My step-step-children (long story), Kevin and Robin, and their wonderful spouses, Suzanne and Tim; my grandchildren, Grant, Natalie, Glen, Emma, Tyler, and Cody; my nephew Steve and his beautiful family, Christie, Cason, and Reese; and my sister-in-law Lyn, for showing me that cooking is family.

My new Tahoe "family," for showing me that cooking is community.

And to my husband, Myles, Carnivorous Maximus, for showing me that cooking is collaborative, inclusive of many different eating paths, and part of a partnership. Thanks for making the sacrifice of being my main taste tester for meals that contained absolutely no meat. This book would never have happened without your input and unwavering support when I most needed it.

Finally, many thanks to both Ina DePaoli and Dorothy Reinhold for helping to test the recipes, and to my editorial team at Callisto Media—Marthine Satris, Stacy Wagner-Kinnear, Maria Vlasak, and Erum Khan—for teaching me how cooking and blogging can translate into a cookbook!

ABOUT THE AUTHOR

Two weeks after leaving the business world, Susan Pridmore traded in her Ferragamos for kitchen clogs. She entered culinary school in San Francisco to pursue a longtime love of cooking. Susan is a mostly vegetarian (Wimpy Vegetarian) married to a mostly carnivore (Carnivorous Maximus), and is on a constant hunt for healthy, delicious recipes they'll both love. She launched her blog *The Wimpy Vegetarian* in 2011 to marry her love of cooking with her passion for writing and photography. On her blog, she shares recipes that can be easily adjusted for multiple dietary preferences. Thankfully, the family dog, Paprika, will eat anything.

BLOG: thewimpyvegetarian.com
FACEBOOK: facebook.com/TheWimpyVegetarian
INSTAGRAM: @wimpyvegetarian

CPSIA information can be obtained
at www.ICGtesting.com
Printed in the USA
LVHW01s0456030718
582509LV00001B/1/P